Betty Jo

Psalm 107

He (God) sent His word (Jesus) & healed them, and delivered them from their destruction.

God is still in the business of healing people spirit, soul, & body. The only requirement is faith in God & His word. I encourage you to take God at His word, find 2-3 witnesses from scripture, & dare to believe & take hold of all He has for you in Jesus!

Blessings

Mike Vidaurri

HE HEALED THEM <u>ALL</u>

31 DAYS IMMERSED IN GOD'S HEALING POWER

MICHAEL VIDAURRI, D. MIN.

OTHER BOOKS BY MICHAEL VIDAURRI:

Handfuls On Purpose

Living Victory

Great & Precious Promises

Standing Between Your AMEN & Hallelujah

Answered Prayer Now!

A Historical Look At Bold Faith & Answered Prayer

AUTHOR'S NOTE: Some names of persons mentioned in this book have been changed to protect privacy; any similarity between individuals described in this book to individuals known to readers is purely coincidental.

Foreword

Everything works by faith. EVERYTHING! Salvation, health, healing, prosperity; all of it works by faith. "And without faith it is impossible to please God, because anyone who comes to Him must believe that He exists and that He rewards those who earnestly seek Him" (Hebrews 11:6).

What is faith? It is a **<u>conscious decision</u>** to believe whatever God has said, **over and above EVERYTHING** else that you can see, hear, feel, touch, smell and think in this life! And, in my humble opinion it is the hardest thing we're called to do! But that's our "job"! Jesus said, "The work of God **IS** this: **TO BELIEVE** in the One He has sent." (John 6:29).

It is extremely difficult to believe in healing when a doctor tells you or a beloved member of your family, that you, or they, have a terminal disease and have only a couple of months to live. Or, you've lost your job, have no savings and the repo man has snatched your car and the bank is coming for your house.

If you don't already have a close personal relationship with Jesus when you're feeling the horrific pain, loss, or fear, it is seemingly impossible to ignore those symptoms and stand on a sentence like: "By His stripes you were healed" (Isaiah 53: 4) written on a page in the Bible. You **FEEL** the pain/loss, **THAT'S REAL**, not some words on a page!

I know that for a fact because back in the early 1980's I came down with what my doctor said was the most severe case of pink eye he'd ever seen—which occurred because I'd never had it before, didn't know what it was, and kept working, putting off a doctor's visit, thinking it would go away on its own! Talk about pain! Oh, my goodness! I couldn't see anything—I had to keep my eyes closed and a warm damp washcloth over my eyes for an entire week!

On my second day at home, basically in bed, because I couldn't open my eyes to do anything—couldn't go to work, couldn't watch TV, sew, read, couldn't even walk around because I couldn't watch where I was going! Now, I'm one of those people who stays busy doing something all the time, so this was not only horrifically painful, it was driving me up the wall because I couldn't do anything! I complained over the telephone about all of it to a friend who was a Believer.

She said, "You believe in Jesus, right?"

I said, "Of course!"

And I was telling the truth, but I honestly didn't know much about Him except what I'd learned as an adolescent in a couple of exposures to vacation Bible School.

"Well, do you believe His Word?"

Uh oh! That stumped me for a minute but, of course, if I believed in Jesus, then I believed in what He said, right?

So, I hesitantly answered, "Oh, yes!" Hoping she wouldn't ask me what He'd said because I would have failed that test! I'd never actually read the Bible and only showed up at church on special occasions like Christmas and Easter.

My friend followed up with "Well, Isaiah 53:4-5 says you **ARE** healed by the stripes He received on the cross, and 1 Peter 2:24 says you **WERE** healed as a result of those stripes on that day 2000 years ago. That's God's Word, past and present tense. He has already healed you, you just have to believe and receive it by faith.

I was silent a minute. My lightning fast mind just couldn't process what she meant. I said, "Well, I've got a horrible case of pink eye. It's obvious I'm **NOT** healed!" Then I waited for her to explain what she was trying to say.

She continued, "Well, you have to **BELIEVE AND RECEIVE** the words that Jesus speaks **BEFORE** you can **HAVE** the results!"

"How can I do that when I'm in such pain, can't see, can't do anything?" I moaned.

She did her best, but I was so ignorant of Biblical things, I just couldn't get it! I tried though! For the next day and a half, I said out loud many times, "*By His stripes I was Healed! I'm healed in the name of Jesus! I don't have pain, I can see, I don't have pink eye!* But all the while the thoughts running through my mind were, *My eyes HURT, they are almost swollen shut, I'm bored, Who am I kidding? I'm not healed! I'm lying! How can I make it go away by just saying words? It ain't true, I'm hurting and I'm sick!* **So, I gave up**.

Five days later I was finally getting back to normal but there was a problem. I kept thinking about it. I DID believe in Jesus, BUT, if what He said about healing didn't apply to us in this day and age, then how could I or anyone else believe **ANYTHING** He said? I had heard the scripture "Jesus Christ is the same yesterday and today and forever" (Hebrews 13:8). And I knew there were plenty of places in the Bible where He had healed people of many things, even terminal diseases. And if it **DID** apply to us, how could I grab hold of it?! What was the truth? Was this just fairy tale, wishful thinking? Could I really stay well when others around me were coming down with all kinds of things? I wrestled with that for a while.

Then it occurred to me that if I wanted to learn more about what He'd said, how it worked, and how to get on board with His Word and stay healed, then I needed to read the Bible! (Like I said: lightning fast brain!)

So, I began with the New Testament. And it took a while. I listened to CD's, and DVD's from various pastors who believed in healing. I watched pastors on television and I started back to church. The entire time I was reading, listening, and learning, I continually thanked God that what had gotten me started was **ONLY** a bout of severe pink eye— what if it had been something much more serious? I could have been in HUGE TROUBLE, because it usually takes a while to learn what you need to know to build your faith and put it to work!

Can you put it to work faster than I did? YES, YOU CAN!

"**. . . with God all things are possible.**" (Matthew 19:26). But you've got to get serious and be tenacious!

And I can testify IT WORKS! I've used it over and over with victorious results for many years now, in all kinds of situations. I still have to fight for it, which means each time I have to make that decision that no matter what, I'm gonna believe Jesus' Word. And it still isn't easy, but it is **MUCH EASIER THAN IT WAS** back with the episode of pink eye! **But you've got to stay in the Word to keep your faith strong and working. You've got to LIVE IT every day.** That doesn't mean you can't do the other things in your life that you need to do, like work, love and play with family, enjoy your hobbies, participate in entertainment, etc. It just means that you spend some time every day in The Word, so you can keep learning and building your faith.

But, someone may ask, "What about someone who has a terrible diagnosis, doesn't know the Word or Jesus, and doesn't have much time left?

The answer: turn off the TV, radio, iPad, and everything else that all of us waste precious time on, and devote your time to reading the New Testament—the first four books tell you all about Jesus, the miraculous healings He performed, faith; everything you need to know, to be able to grab hold of His promises and put them to work in your life. Then go on to the other books in the New Testament.

Afterwards, go back to Genesis and read the Old Testament. Use this book or any of Michael Vidaurri's other devotionals every day. Pick up his detailed book, *Answered Prayer NOW!* There's a WEALTH OF INFORMATION in that book!

Watch and listen to pastors who believe in healing. Read Dodie Osteen's book about how she used her faith to get healed of terminal cancer after being told there was no hope and she'd be dead in just a few weeks.

Contact Moore Life Ministries and ask them for the list of 100 healing scriptures they've taken straight from the Bible—that will help you get the healing Word in you immediately—I read them out loud on a regular basis.

Ask for their FREE CD set titled *God's Will to Heal*. It has a couple of dozen wonderful CD's on healing. The ministry will mail it to you for nothing. I listen to it as I fall asleep at night or at times when I wake up in the middle of the night fighting doubt and fear.

You, me and everyone else, have all been given a "measure" or "grain" of faith. (Romans 12:3). All we have to do is feed it daily with the Word and it will grow. "So, then faith comes by hearing and hearing by the Word of God." (Romans 10:17).

If you will do these things, you too, can say to a mountain,

"Be removed and be cast into the sea…and it will obey you" (Mark 11:23).

But do not allow doubt to creep in—cast that doubt out and decide to **BELIEVE GOD.** Mark 11:24 continues: "Therefore I say to you, whatever things you ask when you pray, believe that you receive them, and you will have them."

Linda Horton,

Author of: *From Hell To Hallelujah!*, *Everyday Blessings and Miracles*, *Fear Not*, *Only Believe*, *Time & Again*, and *Time Will Tell*.

Introduction

God's will **_IS_** HEALING—WHOLENESS in every area of YOUR life! His will is perfect soundness in your body, in your relationships, in your mind, your emotions, and yes, even in your finances.

Psalm 34:10 (AMP) says, "The young lions lack food and suffer hunger, but they who seek (inquire of and require) the Lord [by right of their need and on the authority of His Word], none of them shall lack **_ANY_** [good] beneficial thing." (Emphasis Added).

Is having the ability to pay your bills a "good" thing? Is being healthy and whole in your body, marriage, and emotions, "beneficial"? OF COURSE! Moreover, it's God's will for your life.

In Acts 10:38 we are told, "How God anointed Jesus of Nazareth with the Holy Spirit and with power, **_who went about doing good and healing ALL who were oppressed by the devil_**, for God was with Him."

In Matthew 12: 15 we read, "He [Jesus] withdrew from there. And great multitudes followed Him, **_and He healed them ALL_**.

Luke 6:19 says, "And the whole multitude sought to touch Him, for power went out from Him **_and healed them ALL_**."

One of my favorite Scriptures, Psalm 107:20 declares, "He sent His word **_and healed them_**, and delivered them from their destructions." God's healing is available for you today! Will you accept this truth regarding God's will for your healing by faith today? Will you stand with all those who have freely received His immeasurable grace and BE MADE WHOLE? I pray that today is your day to believe and receive in Jesus' mighty name. AMEN.

Table of Contents

Day 1
He Healed Them <u>ALL</u>...

"How God anointed Jesus of Nazareth with the Holy Spirit and with
power, who went about doing good and healing all who were
oppressed by the devil, for God was with Him."

Acts 10:38

God's will is healing! The Bible is jam packed with scriptural promises concerning the finished work of Jesus and what we have received as His joint-heirs. Healing, wholeness, perfect soundness, spirit, soul, and body is included in our inheritance. Does that mean trials and sickness never come our way? Of course not! We live in a fallen and sin riddled world, but our number one job as believers in Christ, is to recognize who we are **IN HIM** and every iota of the curse that we have been delivered from.

Galatians 3:13-14, 29 (AMP) tells us, "13 Christ purchased our freedom [redeeming us] from the curse (doom) of the Law [and its condemnation] by [Himself] becoming a curse for us, for it is written [in the Scriptures], Cursed is everyone who hangs on a tree (is crucified); 14 To the end that through [their receiving] Christ Jesus, the blessing [promised] to Abraham might come upon the Gentiles, so that we through faith might [all] receive [the realization of] the promise of the [Holy] Spirit...29 And if you belong to Christ [are in Him Who is Abraham's Seed], then you are Abraham's offspring and [spiritual] heirs according to promise."

So, what does that mean to us? It means, if we have received Jesus as Lord and Savior, we are no longer slaves to sin. We may live in a world infected with sin and riddled with sickness and disease, but we don't have to be controlled by sin and its limitations.

Jesus said it this way in John 17:13-17 (AMP), "13 And now I am coming to You; I say these things while I am still in the world, so that My joy may be made full and complete and perfect in them [that they may experience My delight fulfilled in them, that My enjoyment may be perfected in their own souls, that they may have My gladness within them, filling their hearts]. 14 I have given and delivered to them Your word (message) and the world has hated them, because they are not of the world [do not belong to the world], just as I am not of the world. 15 I do not ask that You will take them out of the world, but that You will keep and protect them from the evil one. 16 They are not of the world (worldly, belonging to the world), [just] as I am not of the world. 17 Sanctify them [purify, consecrate, separate them for Yourself, make them holy] by the Truth; Your Word is Truth. (Emphasis Added).

There are a number of things that I want you to see and understand from this powerful passage. First of all, Jesus wants all who belong to Him through faith to experience HIS JOY, HIS DELIGHT, HIS ENJOYMENT, and HIS GLADNESS. That is a powerful statement. Let me ask you a question: Is Jesus subject to sin sickness, disease, lack, or any other part of the curse? Definitely not! Those things can't stick to Him because of His righteousness and they can't stick to you either because He's MADE YOU the righteousness of God IN HIM.

"For He made Him who knew no sin to be sin for us, that we might become the righteousness of God in Him." (2 Corinthians 5:21). Jesus became cancer on the cross so that you could become the Healed in the earth. He became diabetes on the cross so that you could become perfectly sound in your body. He took poverty, rage, fear, sickness, disease, homosexuality, lying, greed, and every other curse from the pit of hell upon Himself, so that you could live free from their effects in this world.

I can prove it from Scripture. When He allowed Himself to become the payment for ALL sin: past, present, and future, that sin physically changed His appearance so that He no longer looked like a man.

[13] Behold, My Servant shall deal prudently; He shall be exalted and extolled and be very high. [14] Just as many were astonished at you, **so His visage [His appearance, His form] was marred more than any man, and His form more than the sons of men.** (Isaiah 42:13-14).

In other words, the sin that He took upon Himself literally twisted and ravaged His body inside and out. He felt the pain and the full effect of the curse so that we could be delivered from it forever.

Hebrews 4:15 declares, "For we do not have a High Priest who cannot sympathize with our weaknesses [human frailty], but was in all points tempted as we are, yet without sin."

The writer of Hebrews isn't just speaking figuratively—he's not speaking allegorically—NO! Jesus suffered EVERYTHING on that cross that man has ever been faced with due to the curse. And He did it so that you and I wouldn't have to.

You may have heard stories of someone who has suffered from sickness and disease say that they are, "suffering for Jesus," as if He could ever receive glory through their suffering. But I want to be clear—that is religious stupidity! There is no such thing as suffering for Jesus! He's already suffered far more than any of us could ever imagine and He did it for us on the cross, once and for all, to deliver us from EVERY SYMPTOM of sin and the curse.

We gain a clearer understanding of this freedom Jesus provided to us when we look at John 17:14-15 in The Message Bible. Here we read, "I gave them your word; the godless world hated them because of it, *because they didn't join the world's ways, just as I didn't join the world's ways.* I'm not asking that you take them out of the world but that you guard them from the Evil One. *They are no more defined by the world than I am defined by the world.* (Emphasis Added).

Hallelujah! What a powerful and awe-inspiring statement! Do you understand what Jesus is saying here? To be "defined" by something is to be: characterized by, limited by, or to be marked by a boundary. Jesus was saying that He had set us free from all of the restrictions, limitations, boundaries, and norms of this world. In other words, unsaved people may be limited by sickness, disease, lack, etc., but not those of us who have been REDEEMED from the CURSE through salvation in Jesus! We live under a different set of rules and norms. We live under Heaven's Blessing—which operates under a higher authority than this fallen world! Praise Jesus!

Jesus told us that we would face challenges in this life because we live in a fallen sin-infected world, but He also said, "These things I have spoken to you, that *IN ME* you may have peace. In the world you will have tribulation; but be of good cheer, I have overcome the world." (Emphasis Added).

So, the next time sickness, lack, debt, or any other part of the curse come knocking on your door—DON'T JOIN IN! You have been redeemed from it *ALL.*

Just as Acts 10:38 declares, "God anointed Jesus of Nazareth with the Holy Spirit and with power, who went about doing good *AND HEALING ALL* who were oppressed by the devil, for God was with Him." (Emphasis Added).

God's will *IS* to see you BLESSED, DELIVERED, HEALED, WHOLE, and lacking nothing beneficial- -in Jesus' name.

When Satan and his minion try to push the curse on you—remind them that you have been set free because of your position IN CHRIST! Let them know that everything must bow to the name of JESUS! (See Philippians 2:10). Confess it loud and make it clear that you understand God's will is for your good and that Jesus has (PRESENT TENSE) HEALED ALL who were oppressed of the devil—and that includes you!

When you do, you enforce the fact that just as nothing could stick to Jesus—It can't stick to you either. If you believe God's covenant Word and stand on the truth that you've been redeemed, sickness and disease MUST FLEE! Jesus has already paid the price for your deliverance from EVERY Curse when He hung on the Cross of Calvary. So, make Jesus proud and receive your healing today. YOU ARE THE HEALED OF THE LORD! Hallelujah!

Daily Declaration

Father, in the name of Jesus, I receive my healing TODAY. Not partial healing, but complete and total healing in every cell of my body, tissue, organ, ligament, blood vessels, and bones. I have been redeemed from the curse through Jesus, and I demand (enforce) my covenant rights as a child of God to be free from ALL of the effects of the curse, in Jesus' mighty name!

Jesus precious blood was shed for me! If I was the only person in the world, He would have died for me still. I am precious to you Father, and I am convinced of Your profound love for me. I am the beloved of my Father! Jesus made it perfectly clear in John 17:23, that You love me as much as you love your "Beloved Son" Jesus. (See Matt. 3:17; Matt. 17:5; Luke 3:22; Luke 9:35; 2 Pet. 1:17).

Father, I am fully persuaded of the love you have for me. I have confidence and assurance of your love. And as a result, I put my trust in You and believe by faith that You want me complete, whole, and sound. Because of this truth, I receive my healing and deliverance by faith NOW, in Jesus' name!

I declare boldly, "I AM THE HEALED OF THE LORD JESUS! Sickness and disease have no legal right to remain in my body. Double jeopardy applies in the spiritual realm just as it does in the natural realm. This law ensures that a person cannot legally be tried for the same crime twice. And since Jesus died in my place on the Cross of Calvary, I AM REDEEMED and absolved of all the just penalties and debts that my sins demand, through His glorious sacrifice. AMEN!

Day 2
It Is NEVER Too Late With God!

" ²¹ Now Martha said to Jesus, "Lord, if You had been here, my brother would not have died. ²² But even now I know that whatever You ask of God, God will give You." ²³ Jesus said to her, "Your brother will rise again." ²⁴ Martha said to Him, "I know that he will rise again in the resurrection at the last day." ²⁵ Jesus said to her, "I am the resurrection and the life. He who believes in Me, though he may die, he shall live."

John 11:21-25

I was encouraged and challenged this morning while reading John chapter 11, and the story of Jesus raising Lazarus from the dead. We often look at things from a "no-hope standpoint" or an "it's too late perspective."

Look at Martha's and Mary's responses to Jesus when He arrived after Lazarus' death: "Now Martha said to Jesus, "Lord, if You had been here, my brother would not have died." (John 11:21).

"Then, when Mary came where Jesus was, and saw Him, she fell down at His feet, saying to Him, "Lord, if You had been here, my brother would not have died."" (John 11:32).

When we experience difficult times we often do the same thing Martha did. We say things like: God if you would have just done this or that before I ended up here...then I wouldn't be in the situation I'm in.

Martha believed Jesus would do the right thing in "His timing," sometime in the sweet by and by. She had faith that Lazarus would one day rise again, but her brothers' death, was THE END – here in this world for Lazarus, at least in her mind.

We know this was what Martha believe because she said, "But even now I know that whatever You ask of God, God will give You." Jesus said to her, "Your brother will rise again." Martha said to Him, *"I know that he will rise again in the resurrection at the last day."* Jesus said to her, "I am the resurrection and the life. He who believes in Me, though he may die, he shall live." (John 11:22-25, Emphasis Added).

WOW! What faith! Martha knew Jesus was the Messiah! She believed that if Jesus asked the Father for anything, it would be done. But she put God in a box.

We often put God in a box too. We get it in our minds that our circumstances are bigger than our Almighty God. We begin to believe that God is limited by space and time. We envision the death of a thing as the end, when in reality, it may just be the beginning of something bigger and better—an opportunity for God to do the impossible in our presence.

What Jesus did next, rocked their world and brought many unbelievers into the Kingdom of God. Like the blind man in John chapter 9, these people were once blind but now they began to see the truth of who Jesus was through this miracle. And their eternal destinations were changed forever when they put their faith in Jesus as the result of witnessing a miracle.

I am encouraged today to recognize that God is so much bigger than my present circumstances. I have been reminded that even though things may "look dead in the natural," that I don't have to wait until I get to heaven to experience the "GREATER" that I desire NOW! I can have it right here—RIGHT NOW—if I will just dare to believe and put my faith in the One who has the power to give life to the dead and call those things that are not as though they were (See Romans 4:17).

God is bigger than anything you and I are facing today. Don't wait until you get to Heaven to receive your healing. Put your faith in Him NOW, and receive your miracle TODAY—it's never too late in Jesus' name!!!

Daily Declaration

Father, I receive ALL that you have for me today! Healing, deliverance, prosperity, protection, security, a sound mind—ALL of it is mine by right of my covenant in Jesus! Thank You, Thank You, Thank You for your sacrifice Jesus! You are the "GOOD SHEPHERD" who takes perfect care of ALL His sheep. You have promised that Your sheep hear your voice, and the voice of a stranger, they will not follow (See John 10:2-5). As one who belongs to You, I believe and listen for Your direction. Whatever You tell me to do, I will do. I am obedient and completely devoted to You and Your Word.

I refuse to let loose of the promises You have made to me in the Bible. I have found in Psalm 91:16 where You have promised, "With long life I will satisfy him, and show him My salvation [Yeshua – the Hebrew name of Jesus]." Jesus, show me Your goodness today! Show me Your healing NOW! I am not yet satisfied with this life and I want to continue in strength and perfect health and soundness, in Jesus' name!

Deuteronomy 5:33 (ESV) declares, "You shall walk in all the way that the LORD your God has commanded you, ***that you may live, and that it may go well with you, and that you may live long*** in the land that you shall possess." (Emphasis Added).

Jesus, I am so glad that I don't have to wait until I get to Heaven to receive my healing and my blessings. Your Word tells me, "Praise the God and Father of our Lord Jesus Christ! Through Christ, God has blessed us [ME] with every spiritual blessing that heaven has to offer." (Ephesians 1:3, GWT).

Since I have every blessing Heaven has to offer, that means I have my healing NOW! Therefore, in Jesus' name, I establish that truth this instant in every cell, tissue, and fiber of my being. God cannot lie, so this must be true! Body listen up: "In the name of Jesus I command you to function and perform in the perfect manner God created you to function!" That settles it. I am healed, and Jesus is Lord of my spirit, soul, and body! Amen.

Day 3
Faith Against All Odds

"[17] (As it is written, "I have made you a father of many nations") in the presence of Him whom he believed—God, who gives life to the dead and calls those things which do not exist as though they did; [18] who, contrary to hope, in hope believed, so that he became the father of many nations, according to what was spoken, "So shall your descendants be." [19] And not being weak in faith, he did not consider his own body, already dead (since he was about a hundred years old), and the deadness of Sarah's womb. [20] He did not waver at the promise of God through unbelief, but was strengthened in faith, giving glory to God, [21] and being fully convinced that what He had promised He was also able to perform. [22] And therefore "it was accounted to him for righteousness."

Romans 4:17-22

During the difficult battles we all question whether or not we're going to make it (even if those questions are never voiced out loud). But I want you to know, as people of faith WE NEVER GIVE UP! WE NEVER THROW IN THE TOWEL! This never give in to defeat mentality, isn't based on who we are -- it's based on who GOD IS.

I'm here to tell you, if you are in the thick of the battle, don't cave in to fear—instead, pick up your sword (your BIBLE), and go for the enemy's jugular!

You may have been standing for your answer for a while now, maybe even years, the odds may be stacked against you, there may not be any hope in sight—BUT FOR PEOPLE OF FAITH— QUITTING ISN'T AN OPTION!

Abraham is one of our examples. Look with me for a moment how he overcame failure and defeat:

> We call Abraham "father" not because he got God's attention by living like a saint, but because God made something out of Abraham when he was a nobody. Isn't that what we've always read in Scripture, God saying to Abraham, "I set you up as father of many peoples?" Abraham was first named "father" and then became a father because he dared to trust God to do what only God could do: raise the dead to life, with a word make something out of nothing. When everything was hopeless, Abraham believed anyway, deciding to live not on the basis of what he saw he couldn't do but on what God said he would do. And so he was made father of a multitude of peoples. God himself said to him, "You're going to have a big family, Abraham!"[19-25] Abraham didn't focus on his own impotence and say, "It's hopeless. This hundred-year-old body could never father a child." Nor did he survey Sarah's decades of infertility and give up. He didn't tiptoe around God's promise asking cautiously skeptical questions. He plunged into the promise and came up strong, ready for God, sure that God would make good on what he had said. That's why it is said, "Abraham was declared fit before God by trusting God to set him right." But it's not just Abraham; it's also us! The same thing gets said about us when we embrace and believe the One who brought Jesus to life when the conditions were equally hopeless. The sacrificed Jesus made us fit for God, set us right with God. (Romans 4:17-25, MSG).

I don't care how many times you've made your faith declarations and not seen any improvement in your situation—that doesn't change the fact that God is at work bringing His promises to pass just like He promised. (See Psalm 138:8; Isaiah 40:8, Isaiah 55:11; Philippians 1:6).

The wonderful news is: our God is the God of the impossible—He is the God of the, "Then Suddenly..." (See Mark 9:23; Isaiah 48:3).

Many Christians may not believe it, but God has you on His mind. In fact, He sent His most precious commodity—JESUS—to bring us ALL back into a right relationship with Him. This act of amazing grace, once again gave us all the legal right to make our requests of Him and to receive answers directly from the throne of grace (a place of unearned, unmerited favor) from God (Hebrews 4:16; 1 John 5:14-15).

If you are feeling weak or battle worn, I want to encourage you today to stick with it and refuse to give up. GOD IS FOR YOU! HE IS ON YOUR SIDE! AND HE WILL COME THROUGH FOR YOU!

The truth is: when God is on your side you can't lose—It's Impossible! You have no choice but to experience your victory if you remain in faith—you have God's Word on it! (See 1 Corinthians 15:57 and 2 Corinthians 2:14). Jesus Is Lord!

Daily Declaration

In Mark 14:36, Romans 8:15, and Galatians 4:6, You revealed yourself to us as Abba Father. You revealed Yourself in a personal and intimate way. You did this because you wanted us to know You not just as ALMIGHTY GOD, but also as FATHER or DADDY. Not as a stern judge sitting on His throne ruling and reigning, but also as an intimate loving FATHER who longs to show His grace and love to His children.

Oh Father, how we long to experience your loving embrace. How we long to know that You are pleased with us and have exhausted Your wrath upon the body of Jesus and have fully received us into Your presence with open arms.

Father, how thankful we are for Jesus our High Priest and Savior, who has MADE US the RIGHTEOUSNESS OF GOD, through His sacrifice on the Cross. (See 2 Corinthians 5:21). There is no more wrath for those who are IN CHRIST JESUS! Praise God!

We are now free to come boldly to Your throne and request ANYTHING knowing with certainty that we have RECEIVED IT, because of Jesus' sacrifice and because of Your unquenchable love for us.

NOTHING can separate me from your love Father. NOTHING! Not any sin, not any wrong thoughts, nothing! (See Romans 8:31-39). I am forever positioned in Your loving arms and graces because of Jesus. And knowing this makes me love You even more. Thank You Jesus! Thank You Father! Thank You Daddy. I rest in Your amazing love for me, in Jesus' name. Amen.

Day 4
Meditate Your Way To
Perfect Health

"[20] My son, give attention to my words; incline your ear to my sayings. [21] Do not let them depart from your eyes; keep them in the midst of your heart; [22] For they are life to those who find them, and health to all their flesh. [23] Keep your heart with all diligence, for out of it spring the issues of life."

Proverbs 4:20-23

The Word of God is alive and powerful! It's not just a bunch of random words written on old parchment by ancient scribes who were bored and looking for something to occupy their time. No! God used ordinary men and women like you and me, who were devoted to Him, to speak to the people of their day and give them a glimpse into God's character – His goodness.

In Proverbs 4:20-23 we are told to "give attention to God's Word, to incline our ear to His sayings." The Septuagint, the Greek version of the Old Testament Hebrew Bible, which was widely used during Jesus time on earth, literally says that we are to, (Gk. *Prosecho*) "turn our minds to," or "take care to pay attention to," and (Gk. *Paraballo*) "to throw our ear towards," or "to offer our ear up to the Lord by approaching and comparing His sayings."

The result of doing so, according to the Bible, is finding life and receiving health in **_ALL_** our flesh. What a powerful promise. Who doesn't want that?

You may be thinking to yourself, *Great, but how do I accomplish this?* Well let me help you. It's not as difficult as it may seem. We do this by meditating on the promises of the Bible.

In Joshua 1:8 we read, "This Book of the Law shall not depart from your mouth, but you shall meditate in it day and night, that you may observe to do according to all that is written in it. ***For then YOU will make your way prosperous, and then YOU will have good success.*** "(Emphasis Added).

The word translated as meditate in our English Bibles is the Hebrew word *Hagah* which means: to murmur, to mutter, to utter, to speak, to imagine, to roar, to talk over, or to meditate upon. In reality, meditation is the practice of giving serious attention to something and fixing your thoughts upon it by muttering or speaking it over repeatedly as a way of studying it.

Through these verses God is telling us that it's not enough just to know about His promises in the Bible, to have heard them in the past, but to make them part of our daily lives by thoroughly digesting ALL of the spiritual nutrients contained in His Word.

In Romans 10:17 we are told, "So then faith comes by hearing, and hearing by the Word of God."

In other words, you cannot live on yesterday's Word just like you can't live on yesterday's breakfast. You must feed your spirit-man daily just like you feed your physical body daily. And feeding consists of more than a casual reading—it requires breaking it down into digestible portions.

Let me give you an example. Have you ever seen a cow chew its cud? If not, that's ok, I'll explain the process. At one time it was believed that animals like deer, goats, sheep, cows, giraffes, etc., all had four stomachs, but they don't. They have one stomach with four distinct compartments. The compartments of the stomach are as follows: the rumen, the reticulum, the omasum, and the abomasum.

When a cow eats grass, it chews on that grass until it has broken it down into small pieces and then it swallows those pieces which then go to the rumen. In the rumen, the first compartment of a cow's stomach, bacteria and enzymes mix with the grass to begin breaking it down for digestion. But then the cow regurgitates the partially digested grass which is called cud, and chews on it a little bit more before swallowing it back down into the second compartment, the reticulum.

The reticulum's job is to separate the good from the bad, or the nutrients from the waste. In other words, foreign object like rocks, wire fencing, or other harmful objects that were eaten are separated from the nutrient rich grass and grains so that the animal isn't harmed.

From the reticulum, the stomach walls then squeeze and push the nutrient rich food to the omasum. In the omasum, absorption takes place. Salt, water, and nutrients are further separated from solid waste and passed to the last chamber, the abomasum. In the abomasum, which is similar to the human stomach, the food is then introduced to stomach acids and enzymes which break the food particles down further, release the nutrients into the bloodstream, and send the waste through the intestines and out of the animal.

I described all of this to illustrate an important process that relates to meditation on the Word. When we take in Scriptural promises concerning healing, prosperity, God's love and favor, or when we meditate on who we are in Christ—we must chew on those truths. Listen, if you're honest with yourself, you know down deep inside that you (on your own—apart from Jesus), are unworthy of anything good coming to you from God.

And Satan, the Accuser of the brethren (See Revelation 12:10), is always quick to remind us of this fact. That is why the Apostle Paul told us it was so important to renew our minds to the truth of the Word (See Romans 12:1-2).

It's also why Paul wanted you and me to know that you have been "MADE THE RIGHTEOUSNESS OF GOD IN CHRIST" (See 2 Corinthians 5:21). Jesus did that for you and me on the Cross because we couldn't do it for ourselves.

When you "chew" on the Word through meditation, you think intently about what God has said about you and who He's said you are. You then begin to see yourself the way God sees you. And soon you begin to say what He has said about you.

I am the righteousness of God In Christ. Jesus bore my sickness, He carried my diseases, and by His stripes I am healed. (See Isaiah 53:3-5, Matthew 8:17, and 1 Peter 2:24). And since I am healed, Satan has NO LEGAL RIGHT, to put this sickness on me! In fact devil, you are trespassing on God's property! Jesus has already redeemed me from the curse of the law, and if He paid the price for my sin, I am free from the penalty of sin through faith in Him! I refuse to remain sick, depressed, in debt, or accept any other part of the curse in Jesus' name! I am Abraham's seed and an heir to the promise of the Blessing IN Jesus! AMEN. (See Galatians 3:13-14, 29 and Deuteronomy 28:1-14).

Now if you've been a believer for very long, you know that the devil is a persistent cuss. In the midst of meditating and confessing Scriptures, he will test you to see just how certain you are you've received your healing. He'll do things like send a sharp pain to the part of your body you just declared healed, to see if he can get you to change your mind.

He does this because he knows the power of confession. If he can get you to doubt your healing and confess that you're sick—then he's won, the battle. Our job is to remain steadfast in our faith and confession of God's Word—in spite of what we may think or feel. Feelings change—but God's Word doesn't! If He's said, "by His stripes you're healed," then you are, it's settled! whose Word are you going to believe?

If you're believing to be debt free, Satan may have a bill collector call you the instant after you've declared yourself free from debt. But don't buy the lie—those tests are meant to cause you to doubt and move into fear. You've got to stay in faith, just like Paul did when he was faced with persecution, imprisonment, and even death for his faith in God.

In Acts 20:24 Paul declared, **But none of these things move me**; nor do I count my life dear to myself, so that I may finish my race with joy, and the ministry which I received from the Lord Jesus, to testify to the gospel of the grace of God." (Emphasis Added).

Don't allow the devil to move you from your position of faith—just keep "Chewing" on the promises of God concerning your situation saying, "With LONG LIFE God will satisfy me and show me His SALVATION (His wholeness, protection, favor, peace, perfect health, never-ending love, goodness, and prosperity) because He is my God and I am His covenant Child. (See Psalm 91:16).

Just like a cow, keep "chewing" on that precious Word of God and suck out all of the rich, life-giving, lie-transforming nutrients that are contained deep within. Continue meditating on the Word all throughout the day until your mind and spirit are built up and convinced that you are healed, whole, delivered, and set free from whatever bondage the enemy is trying to convince you that you are trapped in. He is a liar (See John 8:44). You have been redeemed from the Curse in Jesus!

Your job is to find yourself in the Scripture. Find out what God has promised you through your relationship with Christ, and to feed upon those promises by meditating and speaking them over and over. You've got to begin seeing yourself the way God sees you (picturing yourself healed and whole) even when your outward circumstances don't match what He has said about you. That is what faith is. That's what it means to fight the Good Fight of Faith. (1 Timothy 6:12).

And finally, don't settle for anything less than what God has promised you—COMPLETE WHOLENESS—in every area of life! Jesu paid the ultimate price so that YOU could live!

JESUS DIED A HORRIBLE DEATH ON THE CROSS SO THAT YOU COULD LIVE ABUNDANTLY BLESSED—ABUNDANTLY HEALED—AND ABUNDANTLY VICTORIOUS IN HIM! AMEN!

Daily Declaration

Today, I declare that I will meditate upon and draw out everything that You have for me in Your Word Lord. I am who You have said I am. I take by faith, everything that You died on the Cross to provide for me. And I refuse to settle for anything less, in Jesus' name.

Devil, you are a defeated foe in Jesus' mighty name! you may whimper, and scamper, and try to convince me that I am something other than what the Bible tells me I am, but I want you to know it's too late for that NOW! I am a child of the Most High God. I am the beloved of my Father. And I and Blessed, Highly Favored, and Deeply Loved by Jesus, my Lord and Savior. Nothing can separate me from His love and His goodness.

I have determined to chew on God's Word from this day forth. I will see my victory over sickness, poverty, and death on this side of Heaven, in Jesus' mighty name.

The Bible says in Psalm 27:13, "I would have lost heart, unless I had believed that I would see the goodness of the LORD in the land of the living."

I believe God's promises to me and will settle for nothing less than His best. You may have fooled me before, but not now you slimy cuss! I am Blessed! I am Redeemed! I Am Healed! I am Prosperous! I am a Favorite Child of my Father! And Jesus has seen to it that I WIN! You might as well tuck tail and run, because you aren't winning this battle. This battle is the Lord's and He and I will receive all the spoils of victory, in Jesus' name! Amen.

Day 5
You Have Got To See It In Order To Receive It

"Where there is no vision, the people perish…"

Proverbs 29:18 (KJV)

You've got to see yourself the way God sees you if you want to partake of the divine plan of God. So many people pray continually for the breakthrough they desire, and yet they continue to see themselves in lack, sickness, and in bad relationships. If you want your situation to change, it's time to find the promises of God in the Bible and meditate on those promises until you can see yourself living the way God has promised in the Bible.

Often, when I counsel people about their problems, I ask them how they "SEE" their situation. This is a critical question and their answer explains how that person views their circumstances and whether or not I am ever going to be able to help them overcome their present obstacles.

In other words, if they "SEE" themselves "STUCK IN AN IMPOSSIBLE SITUATION," then no amount of counseling I can do will ever help them, unless I can help them "SEE" in line with the Word and change their mindset.

The Bible tells us in Proverbs 23:7 that as a man thinks in his heart, so is he. Moreover, whatever you believe to be true regarding your situations, no matter how wrong your thinking may be, that is what you will experience either for the positive or the negative.

Job said, "For the thing I greatly feared has come upon me, and what I dreaded has happened to me." (Job 3:25).

If you're expecting to die from whatever ails you—YOU WILL! But if you will put your faith in God, in His precious promises, and dare to believe Him for your healing and deliverance, you will overcome every obstacle that tries to stand in your way.

Luke 6:43-45 declares, "⁴³ For a good tree does not bear bad fruit, nor does a bad tree bear good fruit. ⁴⁴ For every tree is known by its own fruit. For men do not gather figs from thorns, nor do they gather grapes from a bramble bush. ⁴⁵ ***A good man out of the good treasure of his heart <u>brings forth good</u>; and an evil man out of the evil treasure of his heart <u>brings forth evil</u>.*** For out of the abundance of the heart his mouth speaks." (Emphasis Added).

Whatever it is you believe concerning your situation will manifest in your life. You will either focus on the FINISHED WORK OF THE CROSS and draw the BLESSING of God to you or you will focus on the lies of the devil and the always changing "facts" of this world and draw the curse to you—it's that simple. I'm not asking you to pretend that bad things don't exist. But I am asking you to understand that our El Shaddai (our God of More Than Enough), has the power to override and change every negative situation in your life, but He needs your faith to work to line up with His goodness.

Look at 2 Corinthians 4:18. "…we do not look at the things which are seen, but at the things which are not seen. For the things which are seen are temporary, but the things which are not seen are eternal."

In other words, facts are temporary—they can change. They will change if you get your faith in line with the Bible. But God's Word— His Will—will NEVER CHANGE! In fact, God has said, "For I am the LORD, I do not change…" (Malachi 3:6).

I've said all of this in order to lay the foundation for my point. You can and will have whatever you can ENVISION. If you will dare to "SEE" yourself the way God sees you, you will live a victorious life, but in order to do this you must align yourself with the promises of the Bible. I can prove this from Scripture. If you can see yourself whole, rich, smart, strong, joyful, or out of debt, and you can find promises in the

Bible that say those things belong to you, then you can have them, if you will dare to believe it.

Mark 11:23-24 promises, "²³ For assuredly, I say to you, whoever says to this mountain, 'Be removed and be cast into the sea,' and does not doubt in his heart, but believes that those things he says will be done, **_he will have whatever he says_**. ²⁴ Therefore I say to you, whatever things you ask when you pray, **_believe that you receive them, and you will have them._**" (Emphasis Added).

Psalm 37:4 tells us, "Delight yourself also in the LORD, and He shall give you the desires of your heart."

Job 22:28 (AMP) says, "You shall also decide and decree a thing, and it shall be established for you; and the light [of God's favor] shall shine upon your ways."

The problem many of us face isn't that God doesn't want us to have whatever it is we are believing Him for. Our problem is that we often don't have the faith to believe for the things that He does want us to have here in the earth, and we settle for having them only when we get to heaven.

Ephesians 3:20 tells us that God, "...is able to [carry out His purpose and] do superabundantly more than all that we dare ask or think [infinitely beyond our greatest prayers, hopes, or dreams], according to His power that is at work within us."

According to this Scripture—All these dreams and desires we have are on the inside of each of us just waiting to be pulled to the outside, because He is inside of us. Our job is to believe and to pull them out of the unseen realm by faith, so that we can enjoy them in the here and now. Hallelujah!!!

You might be thinking to yourself, *I understand what you're saying Mike, but how do I do that?* You do it by using your imagination!

I know that when I start to talk about using your imagination, many of you immediately think, *He's talking about things that are pretend—fictitious things.* But that's not true. I'm talking about the act of seeing things that are REAL, but not yet manifest in the natural. Let me give you an example.

If I asked you to close your eyes and to count all of the doors in your house you could do it. You would first picture your home, start with your front door, and then systematically and "figuratively" walk through each room of your home, until you counted every door in your home.

What if I asked you to give me directions to a famous restaurant in your town starting from your driveway—simple right? You could do it just like you counted the doors in your home.

What if I asked you to close your eyes and picture a dog? You would most likely picture YOUR DOG, if you own one. But if I asked you to picture a white dog, that picture might vary depending on the color of your dog. What if I asked you to picture a small dog, or a ferocious dog, or a hot dog? The picture changes still, right? You get my point I hope.

Those things are all very real, but we have been taught that using our imagination is childish. That it is silly and a waste of time—that we are supposed to be mature and to focus on "REALITY" or "RATIONAL THINGS."

That is exactly how this fallen world operates. Satan knows how powerful our imagination is and he has convinced and conned many of us into believing that using our imagination is a bad or childish thing, or that it's a waste of time. But do you remember what Jesus said in Matthew 18:2-4?

> [2] Then Jesus called a little child to Him, set him in the midst of them, [3] and said, "Assuredly, I say to you, unless you are converted and become as little children, you will by no means enter the kingdom of heaven. [4] Therefore whoever humbles himself as this little child is the greatest in the kingdom of heaven.

Jesus encouraged us to have faith like that of little children. To have the kind of faith that believes Him for things we can't see based on our knowledge of His character and love for us. Faith that "SEES" the "IMPOSSIBLE." That's what He expects of us—the kind of faith that

"SEES" and believes Him for the EXCEEDINGLY, ABUNDANTLY, ABOVE ALL WE CAN ASK OR EVEN IMAGINE. (Ephesians 3:20).

Matthew 17:20 says, "If you have faith as a mustard seed, you will say to this mountain, 'Move from here to there,' and it will move; and nothing will be impossible for you."

Another way of saying this is: "If you have faith…you will say…and nothing will be impossible for you."

You might be thinking, *If I say what?* If you say what He has already said about you like, "By His Stripes I AM HEALED" (1 Peter 2:24). Or how about, "Everything I put my hand to prospers in Jesus' name (Deuteronomy 28:8)? Or instead of saying things like I'm tired and feeling weak, say something like, The Joy of the Lord is my strength and my youth is renewed as the eagles in Jesus' name. (Nehemiah 8:10 and Psalm 103:5).

But just saying it isn't enough. You have also got to believe the things you are saying, and you've got to see yourself as God sees you. Try this: Pause for just a moment, close your eyes, and see yourself strong, full of energy and vigor. You may need to look back in time and see yourself as you were when you were 20, 30, or even 50 years old.

Whenever I am believing for something, I often put a picture of the "thing" I'm believing for in a frame beside my bed, so that every time I see that picture, I can pause briefly, see myself with that thing, and thank God for providing it for me.

Imagination is just another word for Hope and hope is the blueprint of faith. Let me ask you a question. What does an architect use to build a building? He uses a blueprint. But before he has a blueprint to build from, he must first decide what he wants the building to look like. He has to decide what style of building he wants: Art deco, Mediterranean, English colonial, Spanish, etc. Next, he must decide how many rooms, how large each room will be, the number of bathrooms, and balconies.

In other words, He must IMAGINE or use his IMAGINATION to choose what He wants. Faith works the same way. We must find out what already belongs to us IN CHRIST and then decide how we will have it. Will we have it God's way or will we allow Satan to limit us and to steal what rightfully belongs to us as children of God.

Jesus said it this way, "So ought not this woman, *being a daughter of Abraham, whom Satan has bound*—think of it—for eighteen years, be loosed from this bond on the Sabbath?" (Luke 13:16).

Another translation renders this verse this way, "This woman that I healed is a true descendant of Abraham. But Satan has held her for 18 years. Surely it is not wrong for her to be made free from her sickness on a Sabbath day!" (Luke 13:16, ERV).

She was a descendant of Abraham, who was God's covenant man and our father in the faith. If you are a follower/believer in Jesus, you are a descendant of Abraham too, and heirs to this same promise. (See Galatians 3:29).

Hebrews 11:1 (AMP) tells us, "NOW FAITH is the assurance (the confirmation, the title deed) of **the things [we] *HOPE* for**, being the proof of things [we] do not see and the conviction of their reality *[faith perceiving as real fact what is not revealed to the senses]*." (Emphasis Added).

Do you see that? Faith is taking what God has said and imagining it to be so. I encourage you today, dare to dream BIG, to believe the Word of God, and to IMAGINE or SEE yourself the way God sees you.

Don't let Satan steal what rightfully belongs to you as a son or daughter of Abraham and heir of Jesus. Don't allow the devil to have dominion over you or your circumstances when Jesus has paid the price to set you free. God has made you more than a conqueror in Jesus (See Romans 8:37). Isn't it about time you start living like one.

Daily Declaration

Heavenly Father, today I ask you to help me see myself the way you see me: healed, whole, prosperous, victorious, blessed, free from fear and depression, and greatly loved by You. Help me to envision myself free from all of the lies that the enemy has tried to keep me trapped in. I am Your child: a son or daughter of Abraham through Jesus, and I have a covenant right to be loosed from all that Satan has tried to put upon me. I decree and declare right this instant, "Devil, your time is up! I will no longer tolerate sickness, disease, lack, depression, or any other cursed symptom to remain in my body. Jesus dealt with those things on the Cross and I have been redeemed from the curse (Galatians 3:13-14). As of this moment, I serve you an eviction notice and demand, in the name of Jesus that you leave and take your sickness and curse with you. You have no legal right to anything that concerns me, in Jesus' name! Amen."

Now Father, I stand on Your precious promises in the Bible and declare: As Jesus is, so am I in this world (1 John 4:17). Jesus is in perfect health and sitting on the right hand of Your throne now and so am I in Jesus' name.

Jesus has a sound mind and so do I according to 1 Corinthians 2:16 and 2 Timothy 1:7.

Jesus doesn't lack anything good and neither do I according to Psalm 23:1, Psalm 34:9-10, and Psalm 84:11.

Thank You Father for taking such good care of me and delivering me from ALL my troubles and from EVERYTHING that the enemy tries to afflict me with (Psalm 34:19). I pray these things in Jesus' name, Amen.

Day 6
You Will Be Satisfied With Long Life!

"^{14} Because he set his love on Me, therefore I will save him;
I will set him [securely] on high, because he knows My name [he
confidently trusts and relies on Me, knowing I will never abandon him,
no, never]. ^{15} He will call upon Me, and I will answer him; I will be with
him in trouble; I will rescue him and honor him. ^{16} With a long life I
will satisfy him and I will let him see My salvation."

Psalm 91:14-16 (AMP)

What an amazing promise! If you could just get this covenant promise from your head into your heart, it would destroy all worry and fear that the enemy is trying to cause you. Think about this for a minute—and do what David often instructed us to do in the Psalms—*Selah*—or to pause and think on this truth you've just heard.

Sometimes in the midst of all of the "stress" of life, the running from one place to another, we forget to just STOP for a moment and catch our breath. That's exactly where the devil wants us to live, in the midst of all the stress and chaos. But Scripture tells us, "For God is not the author of confusion but of peace..." (1 Corinthians 14:33).

That said, if confusion and disorder are occurring in our lives, it's not coming from God. That means it's either coming from the enemy or from us allowing fear to motivate us to distrust the God of the Bible. Isn't it time to slow down a bit and get back on track?

If we would just realize that our lives aren't about what we can "DO FOR GOD." Don't get me wrong, there is a "work" to faith, but there is also a "REST" to faith. What I mean by this is that we are never going to earn our salvation by doing anything! Salvation is a free gift that is received by placing your faith in Jesus and asking Him to become our Savior. He has already done ALL of the work. Our job is to receive what He's already done, renew our minds to those truths, and then share those truths with others. Our sharing is the fruit of or the natural response to our love for all that Jesus has already done in our lives. In other words, we love Him because He first loved us. (1 John 4:19)

The "REST" of faith, has to do with becoming unswervingly confident that God will finish/complete/fulfill everything He has promised us. It's believing that He meant what He said in the Bible and that He will make it manifest in our lives just as He promised.

Do you remember what happened when Abraham and Sarah tried to help God fulfill His promise to them? They created an Ishmael (See Genesis 16-18). This single act of "help" has caused centuries of hatred and bloodshed between the Jews (God's covenant people) and the Arabs (the descendants of Ishmael).

As the heirs of Jesus, our position is always to be confident that God will finish what He has already started inside of us. Faith doesn't believe for God's promises to manifest sometime in the future. NO! Faith believes for the full manifestation of His promises the moment we pray! Faith takes hold of the promises NOW!

I love how Paul explains this process in Philippians 1:6 (MSG). "There has never been the slightest doubt in my mind that the God who started this great work in you would keep at it and bring it to a flourishing finish on the very day Christ Jesus appears."

God is willing and capable of making you perfectly whole NOW! And that's exactly what you are supposed to believe for every time you pray—even though we understand that the completion—The finality of our wholeness won't be manifested until we receive our new Heavenly bodies—when He calls us home. But know this for certain: God can heal YOU completely before this happens if you will dare to believe Him for your healing here in the earth. But it will never compare to that glorious day we receive our incorruptible bodies for the rest of eternity.

[50] Brothers and sisters, this is what I mean: flesh and blood cannot inherit God's kingdom. What decays cannot inherit what doesn't decay. [51] I'm telling you a mystery. Not all of us will die, but we will all be changed. [52] It will happen in an instant, in a split second at the sound of the last trumpet. Indeed, that trumpet will sound, and then the dead will come back to life. They will be changed so that they can live forever. [53] *This body that decays must be changed into a body that cannot decay. This mortal body must be changed into a body that will live forever. [54] When this body that decays is changed into a body that cannot decay, and this mortal body is changed into a body that will live forever*, then the teaching of Scripture will come true: "Death is turned into victory! [55] Death, where is your victory? Death, where is your sting? (1 Corinthians 15:50-55, GWT).

Now look back with me at Psalm 91:14-16 for a moment. "[14] Because he set his love on Me, therefore I will save him; I will set him [securely] on high, because he knows My name [he confidently trusts and relies on Me, knowing I will never abandon

him, no, never]. [15] He will call upon Me, and I will answer him; I will be with him in trouble; I will rescue him and honor him. [16] With a long life I will satisfy him and I will let him see My salvation."

Do you see what the Lord is saying to us here? He's telling us that when we enter into a covenant relationship with Him—He becomes our ALL IN ALL. He becomes OUR GOD, OUR DELIVERER, OUR PROTECTOR, OUR HEALER, OUR SOURCE and supply for *ALL* things! Hallelujah!

The word translated as "save" in the English version of verse fourteen, is the Hebrew word *Palat*, which literally means: "to bring out of danger," "to rescue or liberate from harm," or "to provide something promised or expected." In other words, God will deliver, rescue, or liberate you from *ALL* harm and perform the oath He has promised you in His Word. The real question then becomes, Do you know what He has promised you and are you expecting Him to do it? If not, get in the Bible and find some Scriptural promises that give you the proof of God's will for your life.

Next, He says that you will call upon Him and He will answer. Isn't it wonderful to know beyond a shadow of a doubt, that God hears every one of your prayer requests? He not only hears them, but He also goes to work immediately fulfilling them.

1 John 5:14-15 (AMP) confirms this by saying, "[14] And this is the confidence (the assurance, the privilege of boldness) which we have in Him: [we are sure] that if we ask anything (make any request) according to His will (in agreement with His own plan), He listens to and hears us. [15] And if (since) we [positively] know that He listens to us in whatever we ask, we also know [with settled and absolute knowledge] that we have [granted us as our present possessions] the requests made of Him."

Finally, in Psalm 91:16 our loving Father promises us, "***WITH A LONG LIFE I WILL SATISFY*** him, and I will let him see My salvation." (Emphasis Added).

The King James Versions says it this way, "With long life will I satisfy him, and shew him my salvation."

The word satisfy is translated from the Hebrew word *Sabea*, which means "to meet the expectations, needs, or desires of," "to provide length of days." or "to comply with a condition, obligation, or demand of another." That is powerful folks! But that's not all.

The word salvation is derived from the Hebrew word, *Yeshua*. Just in case you aren't familiar with the Hebrew word (YESHUA), it is literally the Hebrew name for JESUS and means: salvation, deeds of deliverance, wholeness, healing, prosperity, help, peace, protection, security, and victory.

So, if we put all of this together, God is saying that when you receive Jesus as your Lord and Savior, He will rescue you from ***ALL*** harm and danger and answer you whenever you call upon Him for help. Moreover, He will meet the expectations, needs, or desires that you place a covenant demand upon and He will provide whatever you need. It could be the salvation of your spirit, healing in your body, prosperity in your finances, restoration in your marriage, or peace and soundness of mind. No matter what you need—HE IS A COVENANT HONORING GOD—HE IS ABLE—AND HE IS READY & WILLING TO BRING YOU INTO YOUR VICTORY—AMEN!

Daily Declaration

Father, today I come boldly to Your throne of grace and thank You for LONG LIFE! According to Your Word, You will SATISFY ME with LONG LIFE! At this present moment, I am not satisfied, and I ask You to not only give me length of days, but to make them like Heaven upon earth.

Psalm 34:12-14 asks the question: "Who is the man who desires life, and loves many days, that he may see good? [13] Keep your tongue from evil, and your lips from speaking deceit. [14] Depart from evil and do good; seek peace and pursue it."

1 Peter 3:10-12 goes on to say, "[10] For "He who would love life and see good days, let him refrain his tongue from evil, and his lips from speaking deceit. [11] Let him turn away from evil and do good; let him seek peace and pursue it. [12] For the eyes of the LORD are on the righteous, and His ears are open to their prayers; but the face of the LORD is against those who do evil."

Lord, today I dedicate my tongue to speaking Blessing—to speaking Your Word only and not the things of this fallen world—the things of the Curse. Help me to guard my mouth and to align my words to the things You have declared me to be.

I pledge to guard my mind and my heart and to follow the directions of Philippians 4:8 which instructs me to think on the things that "are true, whatever things are noble, whatever things are just, whatever things are pure, whatever things are lovely, whatever things are of good report, if there is any virtue and if there is anything praiseworthy—meditate on these things."

Thank You Jesus for being my sacrificial substitution, for suffering and dying in my place, so that I don't have to. And thank You for offering to me EVERYTHING that You have in Your perfect soundness and health. I receive it _**ALL**_ in Jesus' name, Amen.

Day 7
Paid In Full

"⁴ The fact is, it was our suffering He took on Himself; He bore our
pain. But we thought that God was punishing Him, that God was
beating Him for something He did. ⁵ But He was being punished for
what we did. He was crushed because of our guilt. He took the
punishment we deserved, and this brought us peace. We were healed
because of His pain."

Isaiah 53:4-5 (ERV)

Jesus suffered as our substitutional sacrifice and He did it out of love.
He paid the price for everyone's sins past, present, and future. Even
those people who willingly reject, mock, and blaspheme Him and
choose to go to hell. There has never been and never will be a sin
which Jesus has not already paid for on the Cross of Calvary!

In fact, Romans 8:35-39 says, "³⁵ Who shall separate us from the love
of Christ? Shall tribulation, or distress, or persecution, or famine, or
nakedness, or peril, or sword? ³⁶ As it is written: "For Your sake we are
killed all day long; We are accounted as sheep for the slaughter." ³⁷ Yet
in all these things we are more than conquerors through Him who loved
us. ³⁸ For I am persuaded that neither death nor life, nor angels nor
principalities nor powers, nor things present nor things to come, ³⁹ nor
height nor depth, nor any other created thing, shall be able to separate
us from the love of God which is in Christ Jesus our Lord."

Nothing is capable of separating us from His love. He is no respecter
of persons. He died for us **_ALL_** (See Acts 10:34), but when we reject the
free gift of salvation in Jesus, we willingly choose the curse and **_ALL_** of
the negative things associated with it—including hell.

Even though God loves us unconditionally, He has given us the free will to either accept Him or reject Him in the person of Jesus. He will not "make you receive Him or the benefits that come with being in a covenant relationship with Him. He is a gentleman!

Psalm 103:1-5 declares, "Bless the LORD, O my soul; and all that is within me, bless His holy name! [2] Bless the LORD, O my soul, and forget not *ALL HIS BENEFITS*. [3] *WHO FORGIVES ALL* your iniquities, *WHO HEALS ALL* your diseases, [4] Who redeems your life from destruction, Who crowns you with lovingkindness and tender mercies, [5] Who satisfies your mouth with good things, so that your youth is renewed like the eagle's." (Emphasis Added).

Look at all of those wonderful benefits: forgiveness of *ALL* sin. HEALING OF *ALL* DISEASES (it doesn't say only the not so serious diseases, it says *ALL* of them). He redeems us from destruction and gives us eternal life. He protects us from *ALL* harm in the earth. He covers or crowns us with His lovingkindness or covenant love and mercy (giving us things we don't deserve). He satisfies our mouths with GOOD THINGS – That means He gives us His authority to speak the Word and to enjoy His creative authority which has the power to change and renew life—the same power that created this world and everything in it.

Hebrews 11:3 says, "By faith we understand that the worlds were framed by the word of God, so that the things which are seen were not made of things which are visible."

Proverbs 18:20-21(AMP) tells us, "[20] A man's [moral] self shall be filled with the fruit of his mouth; and with the consequence of his words he must be satisfied [whether good or evil]. [21] Death and life are in the power of the tongue, and they who indulge in it shall eat the fruit of it [for death or life]."

That's powerful, don't you agree?

Now look at Isaiah 53:4-5 with me again from the Message Bible translation.

"We looked down on him [Jesus], thought he was scum [a nobody]. But the fact is, it was our pains he carried—our disfigurements, all the things wrong with us. We thought he brought it on himself, that God was punishing him for his own failures. But it was our sins that did that to him, that ripped and tore and crushed him—our sins! He took the punishment, and that made us whole. Through his bruises [His torture] we get healed."

I want you to pay special attention to the last two sentences: "He took the punishment, and that made us whole. Through his bruises [His torture] we get healed."

It says that JESUS TOOK OUR PUNISHMENT, AND MADE US WHOLE—AND BECAUSE HE WAS TORTURED AS OUR SUBSTITUTIONARY PAYMENT FOR SIN—WE RECEIVE HIS HEALING IN EXCHANGE!

Do you see it yet? Do you understand what took place on the Cross? **_ALL_** of the sins humanity would ever commit and **_ALL_** of the rightful penalties for those sins were placed on Jesus, who willfully agreed to pay the price that sin demands—DEATH. But in return, because Jesus was INNOCENT and had NEVER sinned—HIS RIGHTEOUSNESS and everything associated with that righteousness was transferred to us. Hallelujah!

Sickness, Disease, Poverty, Lack, Confusion, Guilt, Shame, etc., cannot stick to RIGHTEOUSNESS!!! It is impossible!

In other words, Jesus took **_ALL_** those sinful things from us on the Cross and gave us the right and privilege of taking His perfect health, wealth, peace, joy, etc. He was our substitution. He paid the penalty in full and gave us SALVATION & THE BLESSING. AMEN!

Look at Matthew 8:17. "That it might be fulfilled which was spoken by Isaiah the prophet, saying: "He Himself took our infirmities and bore our sicknesses."

If He bore them, then why are we hanging on to them—let them go by faith and RECEIVE YOUR HEALING. Receive all that Jesus did for you and live long, strong, and in perfect health in Jesus' name.

1 Peter 2:24 reminds us of this fact again saying, "Who Himself bore our sins in His own body on the tree, that we, having died to sins, might live for righteousness—**_BY WHOSE STRIPES YOU WERE HEALED_**." (Emphasis Added).

If you "WERE HEALED," then you "ARE HEALED" as far as God is concerned! Satan cannot take from you what Jesus made available to you, unless you allow him to do so. Now that you know what you have been delivered from continue to stand on these precious promises and place a faith demand on your healing and anything else that you might need from the Lord.

Jesus paid the price for your salvation (for your deliverance, healing, prosperity, safety, security, and victory in every area of life). Moreover, He stamped both your sins and my sins **PAID IN FULL**, when He died on the Cross. AMEN! So never settle for less than God's Word—HIS BEST FOR YOUR LIFE—in Jesus' Name!

Daily Declaration

Thank You Father for sending Jesus! I am so grateful for Your great love for me. A love that would sacrifice Your Beloved Son in my place— the Son that You love. I love reading that in the Bible.

Matthew 3:17 says it this way, "This is My Beloved Son, in whom I am well pleased."

The New Living Translation states, "This is my dearly loved Son, who brings me great joy."

To think that You would allow Him to be sacrificed in my place is too great to fathom. I love You and thank You for such a great sacrifice. I could never imagine doing such a thing with my own child whom I love dearly.

Jesus, thank You for becoming my substitution. For doing what I couldn't do on my own, and for providing for me all that I could ever want or need. I bless You Lord Jesus. I praise Your holy name and give all that I have, all that I am for Your use. Use me Lord. Let my life be a testimony to Your goodness and faithfulness, in Jesus' name. Let people see how good You are and how faithful You are to Your people. Let my life and perfect soundness, perfect health, be an altar to them, illustrating Your covenant love and grace.

I bless You Jesus, and thank You again for hearing and answering my prayers. Hallelujah! You are so good to me Lord. In Jesus' name I pray, Amen.

Day 8
Reach Out And Touch Him By Faith

"¹⁷ And He came down with them and stood on a level place with a crowd of His disciples and a great multitude of people from all Judea and Jerusalem, and from the seacoast of Tyre and Sidon, who came to hear Him and be healed of their diseases, ¹⁸ as well as those who were tormented with unclean spirits. And they were healed. ¹⁹ And the whole multitude sought to touch Him, for power went out from Him and healed them all.

Luke 6:17-19

Just like the precious people in the multitude spoken of in Luke chapter 6 wanted to touch Jesus and receive their healing—You can touch Him with your faith and receive yours too. He doesn't have to be physically near you in order to heal you and make you whole— He is already living on the inside of you and ready to give you all that you need or desire. He's just waiting for you to ask.

In John 14:14 (AMP) we read, "[Yes] I will grant [I Myself will do for you] whatever you shall ask in My Name [as presenting all that I AM]."

Praise God! That is a powerful statement; Jesus said, "**WHATEVER** you shall ask in His name, presenting ALL that **I AM**." God is the Great I AM. ***NOTHING*** is too difficult for Him, not cancer, not restoring your marriage, NOTHING! (See Genesis 18:14; Jeremiah 32:27; Mark 9:23; Luke 18:27).

Moreover, He left what you can receive from Him up to you. He said that you could ask for WHATEVER—that is a limitless word. He didn't place any limitations on which prayers He would answer or which one He wouldn't. He left what you receive up to you, based on what you would ask and believe Him for. Don't you see He's willing to give it all to you if you'll just ask Him for it?

In fact, no mountain, no obstacle, no sickness or disease, can block you from your blessing if you are willing to ask, believe, and receive it by faith.

Mark 11:23-24 declares, "[23] For assuredly, I say to you, whoever says to this mountain, 'Be removed and be cast into the sea,' and does not doubt in his heart, but believes that those things he says will be done, he will have whatever he says. [24] Therefore I say to you, whatever things you ask when you pray, believe that you receive them, and you will have them."

This truth makes that old Marvin Gaye song, *Ain't No Mountain High Enough*, ring true, at least when it comes to receiving your miracle from God.

> *"Ain't no mountain high enough, ain't no valley low enough, ain't no river wide enough to keep me from getting to you!"*

It reminds me of Isaiah 54:17 which promises, "No weapon formed against you shall prosper, and every tongue which rises against you in judgment you shall condemn. This is the heritage of the servants of the LORD, and their righteousness is from Me," says the LORD."

According to this passage, our responsibility is to know what belongs to us as covenant children of God and to condemn or rebuke any sickness, disease, or negative circumstance that tries to come between us and the realization of God's promises. This authority in Christ is part of our inheritance—it's our heritage.

In fact, Romans 8:16-17 says, "[16] The Spirit Himself bears witness with our spirit that we are children of God, [17] and if children, then heirs—heirs of God and joint heirs with Christ..."

Just in case you're not aware, Jesus does not have any part in sickness. Sickness is part of the Curse. And if Jesus doesn't have it, then neither should you. You have been redeemed from the Curse according to Galatians 3:13-14, 29. You are heirs of the Blessing of Abraham according to Galatians 3:29, "And if you are Christ's, then you are Abraham's seed, and heirs according to the promise."

We can find the Blessing of Abraham in Deuteronomy 28:1-14.

> Now it shall come to pass, if you diligently obey the voice of the LORD your God, to observe carefully all His commandments which I command you today, that the LORD your God will set you high above all nations of the earth. [2] And all these blessings shall come upon you and overtake you, because you obey the voice of the LORD your God: [3] "Blessed shall you be in the city, and blessed shall you be in the country. [4] "Blessed shall be the fruit of your body, the produce of your ground and the increase of your herds, the increase of your cattle and the offspring of your flocks. [5] "Blessed shall be your basket and your kneading bowl. [6] "Blessed shall you be when you come in, and blessed shall you be when you go out. [7] "The LORD will cause your enemies who rise against you to be defeated before your face; they shall come out against you one way and flee before you seven ways. [8] "The LORD will command the blessing on you in your storehouses and in all to which you set your hand, and He will bless you in the land which the LORD your God is giving you. [9] "The LORD will establish you as a holy people to Himself, just as He has sworn to you, if you keep the commandments of the LORD your God and walk in His ways. [10] Then all peoples of the earth shall see that you are called by the name of the LORD, and they shall be afraid of you. [11] And the LORD will grant you plenty of goods, in the fruit of your body, in the increase of your livestock, and in the produce of your ground, in the land of which the LORD swore to your fathers to give you. [12] The LORD

will open to you His good treasure, the heavens, to give the rain to your land in its season, and to bless all the work of your hand. You shall lend to many nations, but you shall not borrow. [13] And the LORD will make you the head and not the tail; you shall be above only, and not be beneath, if you heed the commandments of the LORD your God, which I command you today, and are careful to observe them. [14] So you shall not turn aside from any of the words which I command you this day, to the right or the left, to go after other gods to serve them.

Does this mean that if you blow it and sin it's all over? NO! Jesus has already dealt with your sin once and for all if you've made Him the Lord and Savior of your life. Your job is to repent and get back on track obeying God's Word.

1 John 1:9 declares, "If we confess our sins, He is faithful and just to forgive us our sins and to cleanse us from all unrighteousness."

God's not mad at you and He's not looking for any reasons to punish you. Neither God nor any good parent for that matter, would put sickness, disease, or anything else harmful on their child. Such a person would be called a child abuser. And I can guarantee that God doesn't put sickness on a person to teach them a lesson. That's just bad theology. Moreover, where would He get sickness from—He doesn't have any sickness because it's part of the Curse and God is the BLESSOR not the curser.

Now that we have laid the ground work for understanding how faith works, let me show you a couple of places in Scripture where people actually placed a faith demand upon Jesus and received what they were believing for.

[5] Now when Jesus had entered Capernaum, a centurion came to Him, pleading with Him, [6] saying, "Lord, my servant is lying at home paralyzed, dreadfully tormented." [7] And Jesus said to him, "I will come and heal him." [8] The centurion answered and said, "Lord, I am not worthy that You should come under my roof.

But only speak a word, and my servant will be healed. [9] For I also am a man under authority, having soldiers under me. And I say to this one, 'Go,' and he goes; and to another, 'Come,' and he comes; and to my servant, 'Do this,' and he does it." [10] When Jesus heard it, He marveled, and said to those who followed, "Assuredly, I say to you, I have not found such great faith, not even in Israel! [11] And I say to you that many will come from east and west, and sit down with Abraham, Isaac, and Jacob in the kingdom of heaven. [12] But the sons of the kingdom will be cast out into outer darkness. There will be weeping and gnashing of teeth." [13] Then Jesus said to the centurion, "Go your way; and as you have believed, so let it be done for you." And his servant was healed that same hour. (Matthew 8:5-13).

Jesus never physically touched the Centurion's servant. But Jesus did marvel about the centurion's "great faith." It was the centurion's unwavering faith in Jesus, that placed a demand on Jesus' healing anointing and pulled it out of Him to heal his servant. This man recognized the authority and power in the Words of Jesus. You have those same words in your Bible. Amen.

In Luke 17 we read about ten lepers who wanted their healing.

[11] Now it happened as He went to Jerusalem that He passed through the midst of Samaria and Galilee. [12] Then as He entered a certain village, there met Him ten men who were lepers, who stood afar off. [13] And they lifted up their voices and said, "Jesus, Master, have mercy on us!" [14] So when He saw them, He said to them, "Go, show yourselves to the priests." And so it was that as they went, they were cleansed. [15] And one of them, when he saw that he was healed, returned, and with a loud voice glorified God, [16] and fell down on his face at His feet, giving Him thanks. And he was a Samaritan. [17] So Jesus answered and said, "Were there not ten cleansed? But where are the nine? [18] Were there not any found who returned to give glory to God except this

foreigner?" [19] And He said to him, "Arise, go your way. Your faith has made you well."

Did you catch what Jesus said to the leper who came back to thank Him for his healing?

"Arise, go your way. **_Your faith has made you well._**"

Jesus didn't physically touch these men either; He sent His word to them based on their faith.

Psalm 107:20 declares, "He sent His word and healed them, And delivered them from their destructions." God has done the same for you and me! He's given us His Word. Reach out, touch Him with your faith and receive your healing today, in Jesus' name. Amen.

Daily Declaration

Father, in the name of Jesus, the name that is above EVERY NAME which is named according to Philippians 2:9-10, I take hold of everything You have provided for me through Jesus. I take hold of my healing, my prosperity, my joy, my deliverance, my salvation (peace, security, eternal life, etc.) in the name of Jesus!

I declare that I am whole from the top of my head to the soles of my feet. The joy of the Lord is my strength and I am getting stronger and more joyful by the second. I am blessed coming in and blessed going out. I am the head and not the tail, I am above and not beneath in Jesus name.

Father, Your blessing is hunting me down and overtaking me in Jesus' mighty name. (See Deuteronomy 28:2). No weapon formed against me can prosper (Isaiah 54:17). Satan cannot curse what God has blessed (See Numbers 23:8, 20, Numbers 22:1-14). Therefore, I demand in the name of Jesus that He take his dirty paws off of everything that concerns me, in Jesus' name!

According to 1 Corinthians 15:57 and 2 Corinthians 2:14, God ALWAYS causes me to triumph in Jesus, Hallelujah! I have my victory over sin, sickness, and death now and forever, in Jesus' name. Amen.

Day 9
Living Beyond The World's Limitations

"²² And in that day I will set apart the land of Goshen, in which My people dwell, that no swarms of flies shall be there, in order that you may know that I am the LORD in the midst of the land. ²³ I will make a difference between My people and your people. Tomorrow this sign shall be."

Exodus 8:22-23

Wether you understand it or not, God has set His people apart from the world. As His children, we receive special treatment which we do not deserve, but receive anyway as an inheritance of our salvation and as a gift of His grace. You could say it this way: we receive preferential treatment from God because of our covenant with Him. We have access to things that those outside of a covenant relationship with Him don't have access to.

In fact, Psalm 103:1-5 declares, "¹Bless the LORD, O my soul; and all that is within me, bless His holy name! ² Bless the LORD, O my soul, and forget not all His benefits: ³ Who forgives all your iniquities, Who heals all your diseases, ⁴ Who redeems your life from destruction, Who crowns you with lovingkindness and tender mercies, ⁵ Who satisfies your mouth with good things, So that your youth is renewed like the eagle's."

BENEFITS! Isn't that a wonderful word? There are benefits to being in covenant relationship with God Almighty, Hallelujah! And those benefits are priceless—they are incomparable!

These benefits aren't solely limited to spending eternity in heaven either—even though that would be amazing in itself. But according to Psalm 103, we are promised so much more.

The Hebrew word for benefits is *gemul*, which literally means: requital, benefit, recompense, good deed, or accomplishment. In other words, according to Psalm 103, we receive all that Jesus has taken possession of for us through the Cross.

We receive the reward and repayment of all that was stolen from us through the Fall of Man and the Curse. Psalm 103 lists these benefits that we receive:

1. **Forgiveness** of **ALL** of our iniquities (Hebrew = *awon*), misdeeds, sins, guilt.

2. **Healing** of **ALL** diseases (Hebrew = *tahaluim*), which means sickness, lack of, or to be in a state of famine (without what you need).

3. **Redemption from Destruction** (Hebrew = *sahat*), which literally means: from The Pit, a trap, or from the grave.

4. He crowns us with **Lovingkindness** (Hebrew = *chessed*), covenant love and faithfulness.

5. And **Tender Mercies** (Hebrew = *racham*), which is deep compassion and love which is immeasurable and uncomprehendable by human understanding.

6. He Satisfies our mouths with **Good Things** (Hebrew = *tov*), or goodness or good words, joy, things that are noble (See Philippians 4:8), pleasant things, and everything that is beautiful to enjoy.

7. And finally, God promises that He will **Renew Your Youth as the Eagle's**, which literally means that God will make new and set us high above the world's turmoil and decay, restoring our mortal bodies to the strength, energy, and ease of our early or youthful life.

When I think of benefits, I often think about preferential treatment. For example: there are benefits to flying First Class as opposed to flying coach. When you fly First Class, especially when flying internationally, there are huge benefits. There's more leg room and comfort, better meal options, top-tier service and preferential treatment, and a lot of other upgrades.

Did you know that God gives preferential treatment to His covenant people? He does! In fact, when you ask Jesus to become your Lord and Savior, you give Him the "legal right" to operate on your behalf. He then has the "legal right" if you will, to move mountains of sickness, debt, depression, etc., out of your midst.

An example of this is found in Psalm 91:1-8.

> [1]He who dwells in the secret place of the Most High shall abide under the shadow of the Almighty. [2]I will say of the LORD, "He is my refuge and my fortress; My God, in Him I will trust." [3]Surely He shall deliver you from the snare of the fowler and from the perilous pestilence. [4]He shall cover you with His feathers, and under His wings you shall take refuge; His truth shall be your shield and buckler. [5]You shall not be afraid of the terror by night, nor of the arrow that flies by day, [6]nor of the pestilence that walks in darkness, nor of the destruction that lays waste at noonday. [7]***A thousand may fall at your side, and ten thousand at your right hand; but it shall not come near you.*** [8]***Only with your eyes shall you look, and see the reward of the wicked.*** (Emphasis Added).

Do you see that? People who don't have a covenant relationship with the Lord are dropping like flies all around the one who puts their faith in the Lord and makes Him their refuge. Pestilence, destructions, sickness, war, are raging all around, but NO HARM IS ABLE TO COME NEAR THEM.

Why? Because these covenant children have made the Lord their refuge and fortress and because as their God, He has a covenant obligation to protect, bless, empower, and save them from every symptom of the Curse. Praise God!

The Bible goes on to illustrate that God will change and even rearrange rules, regulations, and laws in order to benefit and bless His covenant child.

Look what God did for Ester and the Jewish people when Haman the Agagite was plotting to kill all of the Jews.

> [1]On that day King Ahasuerus gave Queen Esther the house of Haman, the enemy of the Jews. And Mordecai came before the king, for Esther had told how he was related to her. [2]So the king took off his signet ring, which he had taken from Haman, and gave it to Mordecai; and Esther appointed Mordecai over the house of Haman. [3]Now Esther spoke again to the king, fell down at his feet, and implored him with tears to counteract the evil of Haman the Agagite, and the scheme which he had devised against the Jews. [4]And the king held out the golden scepter toward Esther. So, Esther arose and stood before the king, [5]and said, **"If it pleases the king, and if I have found favor in his sight and the thing seems right to the king and I am pleasing in his eyes, let it be written to revoke the letters devised by Haman, the son of Hammedatha the Agagite, which he wrote to annihilate the Jews who are in all the king's provinces.** [6]For how can I endure to see the evil that will come to my people? Or how can I endure to see the destruction of my countrymen?" [7]**Then King Ahasuerus said to Queen Esther and Mordecai the Jew, "Indeed, I have given Esther the house of Haman, and they have hanged him on the gallows because he tried to lay his hand on the Jews. [8]You yourselves write a decree concerning the Jews, as you please, in the king's name, and seal it with the king's signet ring; for whatever is written in the king's name and sealed**

with the king's signet ring no one can revoke. (Emphasis Added).

Because of God's faithfulness and mercy, King Ahasuerus changed a law that he had established through Haman in order to bless the Jewish people. Moreover, all of the evil that Haman had plotted for the Jews was turned back upon Him.

This is a perfect illustration of Isaiah 54:17 at work in the life of the covenant child of God—the believer. "No weapon formed against you shall prosper, and every tongue which rises against you in judgment You shall condemn. ***This is the heritage of the servants of the LORD***, and their righteousness is from Me," says the LORD." (Emphasis Added).

We have a heritage of Supernatural Favor, Increase, Promotion, Protection, Healing, and whatever else we might need, because we have a covenant with the Creator of the Universe. He will never fail us! God is for us because He loves us! (Romans 8:31).

One of my favorite promises in the Bible is found in Hebrews 13:5 (AMP). This promise gives me so much comfort no matter what I may be facing. It reminds me to live by faith and not by sight.

> For He [God] Himself has said, I will not in any way fail you nor give you up nor leave you without support. [I will] not, [I will] not, [I will] not in any degree leave you helpless nor forsake nor let [you] down (relax My hold on you)! [Assuredly not!].

I pray that you are beginning to see just how much God loves you, how much He desires to see you BLESSED, and beginning to see the benefits and privileges you have available to you as His covenant child. God Is Good and He loves YOU with an immeasurable uncomprehendable love! Amen.

Daily Declaration

Father, I thank You that no matter what I face, You will change laws, regulations and even remove people who may try to stand in my way, in order to see me Blessed! You are a covenant keeping God and I am Your covenant child.

Just like You made a way for Esther and the Jewish nation when Haman came against them to kill all the Jews, You will make a way for me. No devil in hell can keep me away from my BLESSING, my HEALING, my BREAKTHROUGH, in Jesus' mighty name.

I am not moved by what I see, by what I feel, or by the words I hear from so called experts. I am only moved by the precious truth found in your Word—the Bible. I am who You say I am. I have what You say I have. And I will do all that You have called me to do in Jesus' name. You are faithful to complete the good work You have started in me. (See Philippians 1:6). And I will give testimony of Your greatness in my life, for You are good. (See Psalm 145).

I praise You in advance today for my miracle. I receive it by faith in Jesus, knowing that You will never let me down. You have promised that You will never leave me or forsake me. And I put ALL my trust in You. Thank You Jesus! I love You Lord! Amen.

Day 10
None Feeble!

"He also brought them out with silver and gold,
and there was none feeble among His tribes."

Psalm 105:37

Jesus suffered as our substitutional sacrifice and He did it out of love. He paid the price for everyone's sins: past, present, and future. There has never been, and never will be, a sin which Jesus has not already carried upon Himself the "FULL BURDEN" for upon the Cross of Calvary!

In fact, Romans 8:35-39 says, "[35] Who shall separate us from the love of Christ? Shall tribulation, or distress, or persecution, or famine, or nakedness, or peril, or sword? [36] As it is written: "For Your sake we are killed all day long; We are accounted as sheep for the slaughter." [37] Yet in all these things we are more than conquerors through Him who loved us. [38] For I am persuaded that neither death nor life, nor angels nor principalities nor powers, nor things present nor things to come, [39] nor height nor depth, nor any other created thing, shall be able to separate us from the love of God which is in Christ Jesus our Lord."

We've got to cast down thoughts that God is mad at us and that His anger towards us is the reason we experience negative trials in life. God does not teach us by harming us. He isn't a vindictive God who uses our past sins as an excuse to "whip us into shape" in order to help us understand our shortcomings.

I don't care what anyone has told you in the past, if you study your Bible you will find that ALL of God's wrath has already been poured out upon Jesus when He hung on the Cross. That means there is none left to pour out on you.

If you have received Jesus as your Savior, then your debt has been PAID IN FULL! In fact, all Jesus has for you is His love, His Blessing, His Healing, His Provision, and His Peace. AMEN!

The sad truth is that the vast majority of Christians today believe that Our Heavenly Father is looking to settle the score against sin by making us suffer. And many times, that has been translated to mean: "Ok, <u>enter name here</u>, you blew it, so now I am going to punish you by giving you cancer."

NO! There is nothing further from the truth! God isn't looking to "PUNISH SIN." Sin was already punished and defeated on the Cross! We have already been REDEEMED and "MADE RIGHTEOUS" in Christ. That means our salvation has nothing to do with fulfilling the LAW perfectly, but everything to do with making Jesus the King of our lives and receiving His mercy and unmerited favor – His amazing GRACE.

Romans 8:3-4 says, "[3] For what the law could not do in that it was weak through the flesh, God did by sending His own Son in the likeness of sinful flesh, on account of sin: He condemned sin in the flesh, [4] that the righteous requirement of the law might be fulfilled in us who do not walk according to the flesh but according to the Spirit."

Do you see that? Man could never keep the Law (the Ten Commandments) perfectly – it is impossible for corrupted and fallen man to do on his own. But for the Man Jesus, who was born of the Holy Spirit, it was perfectly possible. Because there was no corruption in him.

Did you know that many people debate and argue over the basic fundamentals of the Christian faith? They question the very fact that Jesus is God in the form of flesh. They rationalize and hypothesize over key doctrines including whether or not Jesus was born of a virgin and whether He lived a sinless life.

Those Biblical truths and doctrines may be hard to grasp with our fallen human wisdom and understanding, but they are true nonetheless—and must be received by faith. If you call yourself a follower of Jesus, then you must come to the place where you make the decision to believe **_ALL_** the Bible—even the things that don't make "logical" sense to your understanding.

We can't pick and choose which parts to believe and which parts to throw out. It is either **_ALL_** divinely inspired or it's all garbage. Jesus was either born of a virgin and is who the Bible says He is or He's a huge fraud.

Since we are talking about the divine conception of Jesus, did you know that medical science has proven that the fetus does not receive any blood from the mother during pregnancy? It's true. Though Mary carried Jesus in her womb the DNA forming the BLOOD of Jesus came **_ONLY_** from His Heavenly Father.

Leviticus 17:11 states, "For the life of the flesh is in the blood, and I have given it to you upon the altar to make atonement for your souls; for it is the blood that makes atonement for the soul."

This is of the utmost importance when it comes to understanding the "VIRGIN BIRTH" of Jesus. In his book, The Chemistry of the Blood by medical doctor M.R. DeHaan we discover the following:

> When man sinned, and ate of the tree of the knowledge of good and evil and died – he died spiritually and, ultimately, physically. Since life is in the blood, when man died, something happened to the blood. Sin affected the blood of man, not his body, except indirectly, because it is supplied by the blood. For this very reason flesh can only be called *sinful* flesh because it is nourished and fed and sustained by sinful blood. And since God *hath made of one blood all nations*, sin is present in all of Adam's progeny. For in that one sinned all have sinned.
>
> This very fact that sin affected the blood of man necessitated the VIRGIN BIRTH of Christ if He was to be a son of Adam and yet a sinless man. For this very reason Christ could partake of Adam's flesh, which is not inherently sinful, but He could not partake of Adam's blood, which was completely sinful. God provided a way by which Jesus, *born of a woman* (not man), could be a perfect human being, but, because He had not a drop of

Adam's blood in His veins, He did not share in Adam's sin...It is unnecessary that a single drop of blood be given to the developing embryo in the womb of the mother...the mother provides the fetus (the unborn developing infant) with nutritive elements for the building of that little body in the secret of her womb, but all of the blood which forms in it, is formed in the embryo itself. From the time of conception to the time of birth of the infant **NOT ONE SINGLE DROP OF BLOOD** ever passes from mother to child. The placenta, that mass of temporary tissue known better as "afterbirth," forming the link between mother and child, is so constructed that although all the soluble nutritive elements such as proteins, fats, carbohydrates, salts, minerals, and even antibodies pass freely from mother to child and the waste products of the child's metabolism are passed back to the mother's circulation, no actual interchange of a single drop of blood ever occurs normally. All the blood which is in that child is produced within the child itself. The mother contributes no blood at all.

Isn't God amazing? It just excites me to no end that God has a solution for EVERYTHING! Everything that the devil tries to throw at us to derail God's perfect plan for our lives, is destroyed from the foundation.

Now let's get back to understanding what Jesus did on the Cross and how it affects our salvation (WHOLENESS).

In 2 Corinthians 5:21 we read, "For He made Him who knew no sin to be sin for us, that we might become the righteousness of God in Him."

The New Living Translation says it this way, "For God made Christ, who never sinned, to be the offering for our sin, so that we could be made right with God through Christ."

Think about that with regard to what we just read about the blood. Many people struggle with the idea that Jesus never sinned. But once you understand that He had no sin in Him, because none of Adam's blood was in Him, it makes perfect sense. It also makes Jesus' sacrifice on the Cross all the more powerful.

> [5] *But He was wounded for our transgressions, He was bruised for our iniquities; the chastisement for our peace was upon Him, and by His stripes we are healed.* [6] All we like sheep have gone astray; we have turned, everyone, to his own way; *and the LORD has laid on Him the iniquity of us all.* (Isaiah 53:5-6, Emphasis Added).

> Much more then, having now been justified *__by His blood, we shall be saved from wrath through Him.__* (Romans 5:9, Emphasis Added).

We have been saved from God's wrath! Even though God hates sin, He loves us. Sin has been dealt with once and for all through Jesus' perfect sacrifice! There is nothing left to be paid by you or me, if we are born again believers in Jesus.

I don't know about you, but that makes me want to shout! It also gives substance to the fact that God's wrath has been fully poured out upon Jesus, on the Cross. He became the sin that you and I were, and in return we have become the righteousness that He is! Hallelujah! Since this is true, why would God then put something like sickness and disease on us to teach us a lesson? He wouldn't! It's plain and simple.

In fact, where would God even get the disease to put on us? He doesn't have any! Sickness and disease are part of the Curse (See Deuteronomy 28:14-68). And we have been redeemed from the Curse through Jesus' blood and sacrifice! Hallelujah!

> [13] Christ paid the price to free us from the curse that the laws in Moses' teachings bring by becoming cursed instead of us. Scripture says, "Everyone who is hung on a tree is cursed." [14] Christ paid the price so that the blessing promised to Abraham would come to all the people of the world through Jesus Christ

and we would receive the promised Spirit through faith. (Galatians 3:13-14, GWT).

Look with me at a couple more verses before we wrap this up. I believe that if you understand this and receive it in your spirit, then sickness, disease, and every other part of the Curse won't be able to stick to you any longer! Not only did Jesus redeem us from the Curse but He became the Propitiation for us. I'll explain what propitiation is in just a second.

Hebrews 2:14-17 says, "[14] Inasmuch then as the children have partaken of flesh and blood, He Himself likewise shared in the same, that through death He might destroy him who had the power of death, that is, the devil, [15] and release those who through fear of death were all their lifetime subject to bondage. [16] For indeed He does not give aid to angels, but He does give aid to the seed of

Abraham. [17] Therefore, in all things He [Jesus] had to be made like His brethren, that He might be a merciful and faithful High Priest in things pertaining to God, **to *MAKE PROPITIATION* for the sins of the people.**" (Emphasis Added).

In Romans 3:24-26 we read, "[24] [And all of us] being justified freely by His grace through the redemption that is *in Christ Jesus,* [25] *WHOM GOD SET FORTH AS A PROPITIATION by His blood, THROUGH FAITH*, to demonstrate His righteousness, because in His forbearance God had passed over the sins that were previously committed, [26] to demonstrate at the present time His righteousness, that He might be just and the justifier of the one who has faith in Jesus." (Emphasis Added).

Again in 1 John 2:1-2 we learn, "...if anyone sins, we have an Advocate with the Father, Jesus Christ the righteous. [2] *And He Himself is the propitiation for our sins*, and not for ours only but also for the whole world." (Emphasis Added).

And finally, in 1 John 4:9-10 we read, "[9] In this the love of God was manifested toward us, that God has sent His only begotten Son into the world, that we might live through Him. [10] In this is love, not that we loved God, but that *He loved us and SENT HIS SON TO BE THE PROPITIATION FOR OUR SINS.*" (Emphasis Added).

So now, let me explain to you what this fancy word "Propitiation" means, and tell you how it affects each of us personally.

Propitiation is a fancy word which means, the removal of God's wrath through the offering of a "GIFT" or "SACRIFICE."

In the Old Testament it is expressed through the Hebrew word *Kippur*, which is often translated as atonement, as in *Yom Kippur*, the day of Atonement.

We find an example of propitiation in Luke 18, when we read the parable of the Pharisee and the tax collector.

> [10] Two men went up to the temple to pray, one a Pharisee and the other a tax collector. [11] The Pharisee stood and prayed thus with himself, 'God, I thank You that I am not like other men—extortioners, unjust, adulterers, or even as this tax collector. [12] I fast twice a week; I give tithes of all that I possess.' [13] And the tax collector, standing afar off, would not so much as raise his eyes to heaven, but beat his breast, saying, 'God, *be merciful to me a sinner!* (Luke 18:10-13).

The word translated "merciful," in the English, is the Greek word *Hilaskomai*, which is translated as, "having mercy for another" or "to make propitiation for another." In other words, the tax collector was asking the Father to "do away with," or "to wipe out" the wrath, (even though His wrath was justified), for the sins the tax collector had committed. He was asking for God's mercy instead of His judgement.

Another example or picture of propitiation from the Old Testament Scriptures is found in the ARK OF THE COVENANT which was housed inside of the Holy of Holies.

In Hebrews 9:1-5 we read, "Then indeed, even the first covenant had ordinances of divine service and the earthly sanctuary. [2] For a tabernacle was prepared: the first part, in which was the lampstand, the table, and the showbread, which is called the sanctuary; [3] and behind the second veil, the part of the tabernacle which is called the Holiest of All, ⁴which had the golden censer and the ark of the covenant overlaid on all sides with gold, in which were the golden pot that had the manna, Aaron's rod that budded, and the tablets of the covenant; ⁵and above it were the cherubim of glory overshadowing **THE MERCY SEAT**. Of these things we cannot now speak in detail." (Emphasis Added).

The Mercy Seat is the top covering of the Ark of the Covenant. It is the lid, upon which the two cherubim were positioned. The Mercy Seat, also concealed the Law (the physical Ten Commandments which were written in stone), from the view of both God and man.

The word for Mercy Seat in Greek is *Hilasterion*, which is the same word from which we get propitiation. Moreover, it is a symbol of Jesus, our High Priest who is the propitiation (The Sacrifice or Gift given) to redeem us from our sins. PRAISE GOD!

Under the Old Covenant Law, the High Priest would go into the Holy of Holies once each year and sprinkle the blood of bulls and lambs upon the Mercy Seat. This act would temporarily "cleanse" the Jewish nation of their sins for another year.

For the law, having a shadow of the good things to come, and not the very image of the things, can never with these same sacrifices, which they offer continually year by year, make those who approach perfect. ²For then would they not have ceased to be offered? For the worshipers, once purified, would have had no more consciousness of sins. ³But in those sacrifices, there is a reminder of sins every year. ⁴For it is not possible that the blood of bulls and goats could take away sins. ⁵Therefore, when He came into the world, He said: "Sacrifice and offering You did not desire, but a body You have prepared for Me. ⁶In burnt offerings and sacrifices for sin You had no pleasure. ⁷Then I said, 'Behold, I have come—in the volume of the book it is written of Me—to do Your will, O God.'" ⁸Previously saying, "Sacrifice and offering, burnt offerings, and offerings for sin You did not desire, nor had pleasure in them" (which are offered according to the law), [9] then He said, "Behold, I have come to do Your will, O God." He takes away the first that He may establish the second. [10] By that will we have been sanctified through the offering of the body of Jesus Christ once for all. [11] And every priest stands ministering daily and offering repeatedly the same sacrifices, which can never take away sins. [12] But this Man, after He had offered one sacrifice for sins forever, sat down at the right hand of God, [13] from that time waiting till His enemies are made His footstool. [14] For by one offering He has perfected forever those who are being sanctified. [15] But the Holy Spirit also witnesses to us; for after He had said before, [16] "This is the covenant that I will make with them after those days, says the LORD: I will put My laws into their hearts, and in their minds I will write them," [17] then He adds, "Their sins and their lawless deeds I will remember no more." [18] Now where there is remission of these, there is no longer an offering for sin. (Hebrews 10:1-18).

The Blood of Jesus is POWERFUL my friends! His blood is holy, perfect, and the most precious sacrifice ever given! It has the power not only to cleanse us from _**ALL**_ sin, but also to Heal, and to deliver from the Curse of sin (the byproducts of the Fall of Man through Adam and Eve in the Garden of Eden).

The Bible says, "Love has been perfected **AMONG US** in this: that we may have boldness in the day of judgment; **BECAUSE AS HE IS, SO ARE WE IN THIS WORLD**. (1 John 4:17, Emphasis Added).

Let me ask you a question. How is Jesus? Is He sick? Is He feeble or weak? Is He suffering lack, depression, chronic pain, or suffering in any way? NO, HE ISN'T! He is Healed, Whole, and sitting at the right hand of God, because He has FINISHED the work He was sent to do! And He has delivered you and me from the power of sin, sickness, and the Curse through the shedding of His blood on the Cross as our propitiation! Hallelujah!

And just like the Hebrews who sacrificed the lamb, smeared its blood over the lentils of their doors, and consumed all of the meat (the body of the lamb) on Passover night, before the Exodus from Egypt. The Bible declares that, "He also brought them out with silver and gold, and there was **NONE FEEBLE** among His tribes." (Psalm 105:37, Emphasis Added).

I want you to believe the same thing for yourself. That no matter what you are facing today, no matter what the doctors have said concerning your present situation, no matter how impossible getting to the other side of the Jordan looks for you right now, GOD IS BIGGER THAN ANY SITUATION YOU FACE!

As He is, so are you in this world! He is the propitiation that was paid by blood—PERFECT, HOLY, PRECIOUS BLOOD—to free you from every minute detail of the Curse! Receive your freedom and healing today by faith. Because He has brought **YOU** out with silver and gold, and there **IS NONE FEEBLE** among His tribes. AMEN! Jesus is Lord!

Daily Declaration

Father, I thank You for the precious and perfect blood of Jesus! Thank You for sending Your Beloved Son, The Son that you dearly loved to redeem me completely from the Curse. Thank You for making Him the propitiation—the Gift, and the PERFECT SACRIFICE given in my place.

Jesus, thank You for becoming my Mercy Seat. For becoming what I could never be for myself. For saving me from the just, holy, and perfect punishment, for my sin. YOU HAVE REDEEMED ME and SET ME FREE! You have desired mercy instead of sacrifice. Thank You Jesus! I owe You everything.

I am amazed and overwhelmed by Your amazing love Lord. That You illustrate Your love for me not only through actions but also through symbols. The Ark of the Covenant and the Mercy Seat show me that Your best isn't LAWS—all of the Thou Shall Nots, but Your best is FAITH through GRACE—the Freely you have received, freely give. (See Matthew 10:8). You are a giving and loving High Priest.

Father, I receive Your best—Jesus. And I receive everything that He has made available to me through the shedding of His precious blood. I receive my healing, my prosperity, my deliverance, my freedom from fear and condemnation. Just like You brought the Hebrews out of Egypt with silver and gold and none of them were feeble in any way, I receive my silver, gold, and soundness of body in Jesus' mighty name! Amen and Amen. It's all mine in Jesus.

Day 11
Forget Not All His Benefits...

"[2] Bless the LORD, O my soul, and forget not all His benefits: [3] Who forgives all your iniquities, Who heals all your diseases."

Psalm 103:2-3

There are tremendous benefits to living a life IN CHRIST. The most important of which is obviously spending eternity with Him in heaven. But healing, wholeness, perfect soundness, peace, freedom from fear, confidence knowing that God is pleased with you, knowing that He hears and answers your prayers, knowing that you are continually on His mind, and that He longs to do you good, are just a few more of the benefits we have in Him.

The word benefit comes from the Hebrew word *Gemul*, which means: "good deeds," "recompense," "benefits," "dealings," and "receiving what Jesus deserves."

That is powerful! In other words, Jesus, as our substitute, gave us all that rightfully belongs to Him as a "perfect man, who fulfilled God's Law perfectly." In exchange, He took from us all the punishment that we deserve for breaking God's Law. It's what theologians call "THE GREAT EXCHANGE."

Everything we need, and desire has already been provided for YOU and me, in the New Covenant, and it is received through faith in Jesus. It may not be visible to the natural eye, but it is readily available, just waiting for us to take hold of it by faith and pull it into this natural realm.

Whereas the Old Covenant required that you and I perform PERFECTLY in order to receive from God, the New Covenant only requires that you believe and receive by putting your faith in Jesus and His finished work on the Cross.

[3] For every high priest is appointed to offer both gifts and sacrifices. Therefore, it is necessary that this One also have something to offer. [4] For if He were on earth, He would not be a priest, since there are priests who offer the gifts according to the law; [5] who serve the copy and shadow of the heavenly things, as Moses was divinely instructed when he was about to make the tabernacle. For He said, "See that you make all things according to the pattern shown you on the mountain." [6] But now He has obtained a more excellent ministry, inasmuch as *He is also Mediator of a better covenant, which was established on better promises.* [7] *For if that first covenant had been faultless, then no place would have been sought for a second.* [8] Because finding fault with them, He says: "Behold, the days are coming, says the LORD, when *I will make a new covenant* with the house of Israel and with the house of Judah— [9] *not according to the covenant that I made with their fathers in the day when I took them by the hand to lead them out of the land of Egypt,* because they did not continue in My covenant, and I disregarded them, says the LORD. [10] For this is the covenant that I will make with the house of Israel after those days, says the LORD: *I will put My laws in their mind and write them on their hearts; and I will be their God, and they shall be My people.* [11] None of them shall teach his neighbor, and none his brother, saying, 'Know the LORD,' for all shall know Me, from the least of them to the greatest of them. [12] *FOR I WILL BE MERCIFUL TO THEIR UNRIGHTEOUSNESS, AND THEIR SINS AND THEIR LAWLESS DEEDS I WILL REMEMBER NO MORE.* (Hebrews 8:3-12, Emphasis Added).

Do you understand what God is saying here? Let me explain, He's saying that He has set Jesus as The High Priest to mediate between Him and man. As our High Priest, Jesus, offers a one-time, "perfect" sacrifice on behalf of man's sins, because fallen humanity could not offer a sacrifice that would deal with sin completely.

The high priest under the Old Covenant, had to continually offer sacrifices yearly, because according to God, the system had flaws. Therefore, the Father instituted a holy and perfect Mediator [Jesus], and gave Him better promises (meaning it was a one-time fix all solution that was no longer based on man's ability to keep God's commandments (The Law), perfectly, but on Jesus' ability to keep it perfectly.

In verse 7, we find God calling the Old Testament covenant "faulty," not because God made a mistake, and not because His laws weren't perfect, just, and holy, but because man could not keep the Law perfectly, because he was infected with sin.

Then in verse 8 and 9, God explains the solution to man's problem. He will make a New Covenant which is completely different from the Old, meaning that it's not based on, "If you keep my Laws perfectly you will be Blessed, but if you sin even once, the Curse will come upon you."

You see the Old Covenant Law was cut and dry. And man was completely responsible for what he received from God based on his obedience or disobedience. But under the New Covenant we receive His UNMERITED FAVOR – what we don't deserve, based on Jesus' perfect obedience. Hallelujah!

That is why God says in verse 12, "I will be merciful to their unrighteousness, and their sins and their lawless deeds I will remember no more."

You see, **the punishment for sin is death**. Romans 6:23 says, "The wages of sin is death, but the gift of God is eternal life in Christ Jesus our Lord."

God has punished sin once and for all in the body of Jesus on the Cross. His wrath was completely poured out upon His Son, and because of this, He doesn't have any more wrath for those of us who have made Jesus our Lord and Savior through faith.

Does God still hate sin – Yes, of course! Will sin be punished – Yes, but only for those who have rejected Jesus! Don't you see? Sin has already been punished in the body of Jesus – our Substitute!

¹²⁻¹⁴You know the story of how Adam landed us in the dilemma we're in—first sin, then death, and no one exempt from either sin or death. That sin disturbed relations with God in everything and everyone, but the extent of the disturbance was not clear until God spelled it out in detail to Moses. So death, this huge abyss separating us from God, dominated the landscape from Adam to Moses. Even those who didn't sin precisely as Adam did by disobeying a specific command of God still had to experience this termination of life, this separation from God. But Adam, who got us into this, also points ahead to the One who will get us out of it.

¹⁵⁻¹⁷Yet the rescuing gift is not exactly parallel to the death-dealing sin. If one man's sin put crowds of people at the dead-end abyss of separation from God, just think what God's gift poured through one man, Jesus Christ, will do! ***There's no comparison between that death-dealing sin and this generous, life-giving gift. The verdict on that one sin was the death sentence; the verdict on the many sins that followed was this wonderful life sentence. If death got the upper hand through one man's wrongdoing, can you imagine the breathtaking recovery life makes, sovereign life, in those who grasp with both hands this wildly extravagant life-gift, this grand setting-everything-right, that the one man Jesus Christ provides?*** ¹⁸⁻¹⁹Here it is in a nutshell: Just as one person did it wrong and got us in all this trouble with sin and death, another person did it right and got us out of it. But more than just getting us out of trouble, he got us into life! One man said no to God and put many people in the wrong; one man said yes to God and put many in the right. (Romans 5:12-19, MSG, Emphasis Added).

For those of us who have put our faith in Jesus Christ, it's no longer about living perfectly, Jesus did it for us. We are incapable of living perfectly, because sin is still alive and well in this world. Even though we have been redeemed from the Curse, we have not been removed from this corrupted world of sin.

Does that mean that we blatantly abuse the gift of grace – of course not! We do our best to live a holy life which is pleasing to the Lord and one that draws people to Him. And when we blow it, we repent, and move on.

We don't allow the enemy to beat us up with thoughts of guilt and condemnation, with lies that God is mad at us, that He won't love us or care for us anymore. No! That sin was paid for on the Cross too – it wasn't a surprise to God, so get up, dust yourself off, and move forward, doing what God has called you to do to the Glory of God!!! Amen!

God has not only given you the benefit of salvation in Jesus, but He has also given you His peace to persevere under every pressure and trial knowing He will bring you out BLESSED. He has given you His healing power which is available to you in "precious promise" form and found in His Word – but your job is to meditate on those promises and renew your mind to those truths until they manifest in your body.

Healing is yours now! It doesn't have to take days, weeks, or even months – you can experience it all NOW, if you will have the faith of a child and simply BELIEVE and RECEIVE by faith.

You must call those things that be not as though they were (Romans 4:17). In other words, you've got to get to the place where you believe God's Word, even when you don't see it operating in the natural. And once you believe it, you will become pregnant with that healing and you will manifest it in this natural realm.

I believe that your delivery day is coming very soon. I believe that you will give birth to your healing, your dream—that child you've been believing God for.

Why put it off until sometime in the future? Why not receive it today? God has showered you with His blessings. He has offered you ALL the benefits you could ever desire. Don't refuse them based on your natural circumstances and unbelief. Grab hold of them and BLESS THE LORD, FORGETTING NOT ALL HIS BENEFITS! Amen & Amen!

Daily Declaration

Heavenly Father, thank You for all of the benefits You have provided to me through Jesus! Thank You for preferential treatment in this world. Unsaved people may be limited to the World's ways—they may be subject to the doctor's diagnosis, they may be forced to live under the economic strains and crashes—BUT NOT ME!

Jesus said:

> [13-19] Now…I'm saying these things in the world's hearing So my people can experience My joy completed in them. I gave them your word; **The godless world hated them** because of it, **because they didn't join the world's ways, just as I didn't join the world's ways**. I'm not asking that you take them out of the world but that you guard them from the Evil One. **They are no more defined by the world than I am defined by the world. Make them holy—consecrated—with the truth; Your word is consecrating truth.** In the same way that you gave me a mission in the world, I give them a mission in the world. I'm consecrating myself for their sakes, so they'll be truth-consecrated in their mission. (John 17:13-19, MSG, Emphasis Added).

I refuse to join the World's system and to be defined by its standards and laws. Father, Your ways are higher and better than the World's ways and I choose Your ways for my life. Jesus died to redeem me from this World's limitations, and I receive _**ALL**_ of the benefits He has made available to me through His precious blood. Thank You Jesus! I love You and decree this by faith—In Jesus' mighty name. Amen!

Day 12
God Has Given You His
YES & AMEN!

"For all of God's promises have been fulfilled in Christ with a resounding "Yes!" And through Christ, our "Amen" (which means "Yes") ascends to God for His glory."

2 Corinthians 1:20 (NLT)

The other day I was listening to a message by one of my favorite Bible teachers and he was teaching on the meaning of the word AMEN. I have always understood that the word Amen means: So be it, and is an affirmation or agreement with what has been written, said, or preached. But the truth is: The word "AMEN," means so much more.

The Hebrew word **AMEN**, has the same root origin as the Hebrew word *emunah*, the word translated as **FAITH**, in the English Bible and the Hebrew word *emet*, which means **TRUTH**, and is the root form of the word *emunah*.

In fact, AMEN, in both the Hebrew and the Greek are often translated in the English as: "So be it", "Most assuredly I tell you", "I tell you the truth", "This is reliable or faithful", "You can put your firm trust in what I am saying", and/or "Have faith in and believe what is being said to you."

When Jesus spoke to His disciples, He often made the statement: "Verily, verily…" or "Most assuredly I say to you…" A more accurate rendering of what He was saying is: "AMEN, AMEN, I AM telling you the truth…" or "What I am saying is reliable and trustworthy – So Be It!

In other words, Jesus was telling us that there is no higher truth – or that HE IS THE TRUTH SPEAKING. In today's vernacular He was saying, "I'm going to say something to you that may be difficult for you to imagine or believe because it sounds too good to be true based on your past experiences, but it is true nonetheless!

Now that we understand this, let's look together at 2 Corinthians 1:20 with greater revelation and insight. The Bible says:

> For all the promises of God in Him are Yes, and in Him Amen, to the glory of God through us. (NKJV)

> Certainly, Christ made God's many promises come true. For that reason, because of our message, people also honor God by saying, "Amen!" (GWT).

I want you to pay special attention to the word **_ALL_** in the NKJV above. All of the promises of God are YES and SO BE IT! In other words, God hasn't given us this Bible to bore us. NO! It is a book of Precious Promises, that tells us about our inheritance as believers IN CHRIST! It tells us WHO WE ARE and informs us of the things that belong to us as HIS COVENANT CHILDREN.

Look what 2 Peter 1:2-4 (AMP) tells us about God's Promises:

> [2] May grace (God's favor) and peace (which is perfect well-being, all necessary good, all spiritual prosperity, and freedom from fears and agitating passions and moral conflicts) be multiplied to you in [the full, personal, precise, and correct] knowledge of God and of Jesus our Lord. [3] For His divine power has bestowed upon us all things that [are requisite and suited] to life and godliness, through the [full, personal] knowledge of Him Who called us by and to His own glory and excellence (virtue). [4] By means of these *He has bestowed on us His precious and exceedingly great promises, so that through them you may escape [by flight] from the moral decay (rottenness and corruption) that is in*

the world because of covetousness (lust and greed), *and become sharers (partakers) of the divine nature.* (Emphasis Added).

Do you see that? God has made promises like 2 Peter 2:24:

Who Himself bore our sins in His own body on the tree, that we, having died to sins, might live for righteousness—***by whose stripes you were healed.***

He has promised us this healing so that YOU and I can take part in His DIVINE NATURE—IMMUNE and UNTOUCHABLE by sickness and disease through faith in Jesus and His Word. Hallelujah!

I want you to understand clearly that AMEN is not just a religious word that people say in church or "religious circles," in order to sound holy. No! According to Jewish tradition and revered Jewish Rabbis, When God "Rains down His BLESSING upon the earth—the way a person catches it or takes possession of God's promises—is by saying "AMEN!"

Our verbal "Amen," to a word preached or written promise given to us in the Bible, is like the royal seal that is stamped on a decree from the king of a nation. It signifies not only that it is the authentic and royal word from the highest authority in the land, but that it is "Royal LAW." In other words, everyone must obey the demands set forth in that decree or face the consequences. Praise God!

Have you ever seen a movie where the king dips his signet ring into red wax and then stamps the scroll with his royal seal? That is what I am talking about.

Have you ever wondered why the wax seal is ALWAYS red? It's red because it represents the Blood of Jesus!

Revelation 3:14 calls Jesus the AMEN, "These things says the Amen, the Faithful and True Witness, the Beginning of the creation of God."

So, when you and I say Amen, it is just like signing Jesus' name and complete authority to a check we are writing. I want you to know Jesus isn't poor. The Bible says He owns the cattle on a thousand hills. (See

Psalm 50:10). The streets of Heaven are made of pure gold and there are at least 12 huge gates made out of single pearls. (See Revelation 21:21). Not only that, but God calls Himself the Great I Am. (Exodus 3:14). In other words, He is whatever you need Him to be—your healing, your peace, your safety and security, your protection, your freedom from every bondage!

Let's now turn our attention to a few places in Scripture where people said AMEN and took hold of the promises of God for themselves. But before we do, let's look at a person who temporarily missed it through unbelief.

In Luke 1:5 through Luke 2:20 we read about Zechariah (the High Priest) and Elizabeth (his wife) who were believing God for a child. As Zechariah was serving in the temple and burning incense (in the Holy of Holies, See Hebrews 9:3-4) on the Altar of Incense, the angel Gabriel visits him and tells him that he and Elizabeth will have a child and that, Zechariah is to name him John.

> [11] Then an angel of the Lord appeared to him, standing on the right side of the altar of incense. [12] And when Zacharias saw him, he was troubled, and fear fell upon him. [13] But the angel said to him, "Do not be afraid, Zacharias, for your prayer is heard; and your wife Elizabeth will bear you a son, and you shall call his name John. [14] And you will have joy and gladness, and many will rejoice at his birth. [15] For he will be great in the sight of the Lord, and shall drink neither wine nor strong drink. He will also be filled with the Holy Spirit, even from his mother's womb. [16] And he will turn many of the children of Israel to the Lord their God. [17] He will also go before Him in the spirit and power of Elijah, 'to turn the hearts of the fathers to the children,' and the disobedient to the wisdom of the just, to make ready a people prepared for the Lord."[18] *And Zacharias said to the angel, "How shall I know this? For I am an old man, and my wife is well advanced in years.* (Luke 1:11-18).

This may seem innocent enough on Zechariah's part, but it's not. He has just been met in the Holy of Holies by an angel who said that God is answering his prayer and giving him a son. Zechariah's response is based on unbelief. To paraphrase Zechariah: "How shall I know that what you are telling me is true—we're old?"

The angel responds, "I am Gabriel, who stands in the presence of God, and was sent to speak to you and bring you these glad tidings. [20] But behold, ***you will be mute and not able to speak until the day these things take place, because you did not believe my words*** which will be fulfilled in their own time." (Luke 1:19-20).

Duh! An angel just told you that God has sent him to inform you that your prayers have been answered and you will have a child. You are a "Man of God" who serves God daily, and is supposed to believe. Zechariah's words illustrate that he has no faith to believe for his son John to be born. And because our words have power of either life or death (See Proverbs 18:20-21), the angel shuts his mouth so that Zechariah cannot abort the plan and will of God through his negative words.

John's job was to, "[16]...turn many of the children of Israel to the Lord their God. [17] [to] ...go before Him [Jesus] in the spirit and power of Elijah, 'to turn the hearts of the fathers to the children,' and the disobedient to the wisdom of the just, to make ready a people prepared for the Lord." (Luke 1:16-17). And the Father could not risk having Zechariah's unbelief spoil His Master Plan.

In contrast to the story of Zechariah, let's look at the story of Mary the mother of Jesus.

[26] Now in the sixth month the angel Gabriel was sent by God to a city of Galilee named Nazareth, [27] to a virgin betrothed to a man whose name was Joseph, of the house of David. The virgin's name was Mary. [28] And having come in, the angel said to her, "Rejoice, highly favored one, the Lord is with you; blessed are you among women!" [29] But when she saw him, she was troubled at his saying, and considered what manner of greeting

this was. [30] Then the angel said to her, "Do not be afraid, Mary, for you have found favor with God. [31] And behold, you will conceive in your womb and bring forth a Son, and shall call His name JESUS. [32] He will be great, and will be called the Son of the Highest; and the Lord God will give Him the throne of His father David. [33] And He will reign over the house of Jacob forever, and of His kingdom there will be no end." [34] ***Then Mary said to the angel, "How can this be, since I do not know a man?"*** [35] And the angel answered and said to her, "The Holy Spirit will come upon you, and the power of the Highest will overshadow you; therefore, also, that Holy One who is to be born will be called the Son of God. [36] Now indeed, Elizabeth your relative has also conceived a son in her old age; and this is now the sixth month for her who was called barren. [37] For with God nothing will be impossible." [38] Then Mary said, "Behold the maidservant of the Lord! ***Let it be to me according to your word.***" And the angel departed from her.

At first glance, this account of Mary's encounter with the angel Gabriel may look very similar to the last one we looked at with Zechariah, but there is a huge difference. Mary never doubted the word spoken by the angel—she just asked the question "How?"

Mary knew that in order for a child to be born, a man and woman have to be intimate. And since she was still a virgin, it was physically impossible, in the natural, for her to conceive a child—but not impossible in the SUPERNATURAL. So, she was asking the angel Gabriel how it would occur if not the "normal" way.

Once Gabriel explains how it will happen Mary says, "Let it be to me according to your word." We must remember that the New Testament wasn't written in English, but in Greek. When Mary said, "LET IT BE UNTO ME…" She was literally saying AMEN—SO BE IT!

The Greek word translated as "Let" is the word *ginomai*, which is an equivalent to AMEN and the Hebrew word *emunah*, which if you remember is the word for FAITH. It literally means, "to come into being" or "to be granted."

This same word is used by Jesus in John 8:58 when He says, "Most assuredly, I say to you, before Abraham was, I AM."

To give you a little background to verse 58, the Pharisees are arguing with Jesus about His teaching. Jesus boldly proclaimed in verse 51, "Most assuredly, I say to you, if anyone keeps My word he shall never see death." The Pharisees then proclaim that Jesus must have a demon and say something like, "Who do you think you are? Do you think you are greater than our father Abraham?" And this is when Jesus responds:

Most assuredly, I say to you, before Abraham was, I AM.

A better translation of this verse would be:

"AMEN, AMEN, I tell you the truth, before Abraham came into being [before he AMENED] (*ginomai*) I AM (*ego eimi*) I will be what I will be [I AMENED]."

In Genesis 15:6 we learn what Jesus is talking about in the above passage. Speaking of Abraham. The Bible says, "And he [Abraham] believed in the LORD, and He [God] accounted it to him [Abraham] for righteousness.

The word "believed" in this passage is the Hebrew word *he amin* [meaning that he AMENED] in the Lord, and he was accounted righteous. Hallelujah! In other words, he believed and received what the Lord said by faith, and he was "made" righteous because of that faith. (See 2 Corinthians 5:21).

Do you see it? He took hold of **_ALL_** the promises of God by saying AMEN to what the Father said to him. This statement is reaffirmed in the New Testament in Romans 4:3, 9, Galatians 3:6 and James 2:23.

Moreover, every time Jesus says, "Verily, verily," or "Truly, truly," or "Most assuredly…" He is saying, "AMEN! AMEN! I'm telling you for certain…" (See examples in Mark 11:23 and Luke 21:32).

I pray that you are beginning to see the importance of saying the word AMEN and that you understand it's how believers take possession of the promises of God. AMEN is not just a "religious word" that Christians use to sound holy, but instead it's our agreement and acceptance of all that God has already said about who we are in Jesus – and our verbal confirmation of receiving those promises by faith.

Begin to shout AMEN each time you read verses that promise your healing, your prosperity, a sound mind, your protection, the salvation of your loved ones, and everything else you desire.

Say AMEN, to the GOOD THINGS that your pastor or a loved one preaches to you. Say AMEN, each time you read a promise from God to bless YOU, heal YOU, or protect YOU from harm. They are all precious promises given to YOU by your loving Heavenly Father. They are meant for YOU to enjoy and to possess in THIS LIFE—so take them by faith today! AMEN & AMEN!

Daily Declaration

Father, in the mighty name of Jesus I say AMEN to perfect health and healing operating in every cell, tissue, bone, and organ of my body. I call myself WHOLE in Jesus' name. Body, you listen and obey the Word of the Lord this instant! My Heavenly Father sent His precious Word [JESUS], and healed me, and delivered me from my destruction and demise (See Psalm 107:20).

He sent Jesus, the living Word who went about doing GOOD and HEALING ALL who were oppressed of the devil. (See John 1 and Acts 10:38).

Jesus is not only the Word, but according to Revelation 3:14, He is also the AMEN and FAITHFUL and TRUE witness of the Father's goodness and grace. If Jesus is the AMEN, and I say AMEN to Him, then we are in perfect, harmonious agreement of His will, and His healing power is in full operation in my life:

> [19] Again I tell you, if two of you on earth agree (harmonize together, make a symphony together) about whatever [anything and everything] they may ask, it will come to pass and be done for them by My Father in heaven. [20] For wherever two or three are gathered (drawn together as My followers) in (into) My name, there I AM in the midst of them. (Matthew 18:19-20, AMP).

Therefore devil, no weapon formed against me shall prosper in Jesus' name, and every sickness or disease that comes against me I shall condemn according to my great AMEN [Jesus], because perfect soundness and health are both my inheritance in Jesus! (See Isaiah 54:17).

I say AMEN to my healing, AMEN to my prosperity, AMEN to my marriage and to loving friendships in operation in my life, and AMEN to all that God has for me in Jesus!

Jesus, I say AMEN to you as my Lord and Savior. Thank You for loving me and for delivering me from everything that would try to steal, kill, and destroy my life. You came to give me life, and to give it to me in abundance, to the full, until it overflows. AMEN!

Day 13
Receiving Your Healing Through The Lord's Supper

"²³ For I received from the Lord that which I also delivered to you: that the Lord Jesus on the same night in which He was betrayed took bread; ²⁴ and when He had given thanks, He broke it and said, "Take, eat; this is My body which is broken for you; do this in remembrance of Me." ²⁵ In the same manner He also took the cup after supper, saying, "This cup is the new covenant in My blood. This do, as often as you drink it, in remembrance of Me." ²⁶ For as often as you eat this bread and drink this cup, you proclaim the Lord's death till He comes."

1 Corinthians 11:23-26

Today I want to focus on the power of the Holy Communion also known as The Lord's Supper. It was on the night of His betrayal, that "²⁶ …Jesus took bread, blessed and broke it, and gave it to the disciples and said, "Take, eat; this is My body." ²⁷ Then He took the cup, and gave thanks, and gave it to them, saying, "Drink from it, all of you. ²⁸ For this is My blood of the new covenant, which is shed for many for the remission of sins." (Matthew 26:26-28).

Many people have misunderstood both the significance of communion and have also been led to believe that if they have sin in their lives – they shouldn't partake. This by the way, is exactly what Satan desires. He is the thief that comes to steal, kill and destroy (See John 10:10), and if he can, convince you to stay away from The Lord's Supper, and the power it offers, – he's won part of the battle.

In Ephesians 1:7-10 we read, "[7]**In Him we have redemption through His blood, the forgiveness of sins, according to the riches of His grace** [8]which He made to abound toward us in all wisdom and prudence, [9]**having made known to us the mystery of His will,** according to His good pleasure which He purposed in Himself, [10]that in the dispensation of the fullness of the times He might gather together in one all things in Christ, both which are in heaven and which are on earth—in Him."

The Message Bible says it this way: "[7-10]**Because of the sacrifice of the Messiah, his blood** poured out on the altar of the Cross, we're a free people—free of penalties and punishments chalked up by all our misdeeds. And not just barely free, either. Abundantly free!** He thought of everything, provided for everything we could possibly need, letting us in on the plans he took such delight in making. He set it all out before us in Christ, a long-range plan in which everything would be brought together and summed up in him, everything in deepest heaven, everything on planet earth."

Isn't it amazing? Jesus' blood has set us free from the Curse and has given us forgiveness of our sins! I know, you're probably saying to yourself, *"But Mike, I already know this, that's no big revelation."* To which I say, Yes, but do you really BELIEVE IT?

You see, understanding that **YOU** have been forgiven of ***ALL*** of **YOUR** sins is the first step to receiving **YOUR HEALING**.

[17]Now it happened on a certain day, as He was teaching, that there were Pharisees and teachers of the law sitting by, who had come out of every town of Galilee, Judea, and Jerusalem. And the power of the Lord was present to heal them. [18]Then behold, men brought on a bed a man who was paralyzed, whom they sought to bring in and lay before Him. [19]And when they could not find how they might bring him in, because of the crowd, they went up on the housetop and let him down with his bed through the tiling into the midst before Jesus.

[20] When He saw their faith, He said to him, **"Man, your sins are forgiven you."** [21] And the scribes and the Pharisees began to reason, saying, "Who is this who speaks blasphemies? Who can forgive sins but God alone?" [22] **But when Jesus perceived their thoughts, He answered and said to them, "Why are you reasoning in your hearts? [23] Which is easier, to say, 'Your sins are forgiven you,' or to say, 'Rise up and walk'? [24] But that you may know that the Son of Man has power on earth to forgive sins"—He said to the man who was paralyzed, "I say to you, arise, take up your bed, and go to your house." [25] Immediately he rose up before them, took up what he had been lying on, and departed to his own house, glorifying God.** [26] And they were all amazed, and they glorified God and were filled with fear, saying, "We have seen strange things today! (Luke 5:17-26, Emphasis Added).

This is significant people, Jesus didn't touch this paralyzed man, the man didn't touch Jesus' prayer shawl, the only thing that happened was Jesus said, "Man, your sins are forgiven you…rise up and walk."

Knowing or having faith in the fact that the Lord had forgiven him of all his sins is what led to this man's healing. That's powerful! We can say that we know we've been forgiven, but knowing isn't enough – we must believe it. Why? Because of unconscious or subconscious self-sabotage – the need to maintain good feelings/emotions while reducing bad feelings/emotions. Psychologist call this cognitive dissonance.

An example of this would be an accident-prone female who unconsciously punishes herself because of the guilt she feels for being unfaithful to her spouse. Because of the immense guilt she feels, and because of her need to reduce that guilt, she unconsciously harms herself by repeatedly tripping over things or running into things that most people wouldn't.

I have said all of this to make the point that even though we may understand the truth that we have been forgiven as members of the Body of Christ, we may still have that cognitive dissonance because we feel that "OUR SINS" are too "BIG" to be forgiven of. I believe that is the reason Jesus told this man that his sins were forgiven before he could receive his healing.

UNDERSTANDING THAT YOU ARE FORGIVEN COMPLETELY, COMES BEFORE YOUR HEALING! That is powerful.

Another misunderstanding has been the fact that many of us have lumped both the bread and the wine together believing that they are both for the forgiveness of sins, but Jesus makes a distinction between the two elements.

In 1 Corinthians 11:24 we discover, "And when He had given thanks, He broke it and said, "Take, eat; this is My body which is broken for you; do this in remembrance of Me."

Jesus, specifically pointed to the fact that His body was broken for ours and that we should remember this as often as we partake of it. Why is this?

It goes back to the GREAT EXCHANGE. Why Did Jesus come in the first place? He came to free us from the power of the Curse. He came to restore mankind to righteousness so that we could enjoy God's original intent before the FALL – a loving relationship with Him where we could enjoy the rights and privileges of being sons and daughters in His family.

In other words, Jesus willfully died so that YOU and I don't have to. His body was broken by the effects of sin so that YOURS and MINE don't have to be. He was beat and ravaged by every vile torture that man could dish out (the Roman scourging) and every symptom of sickness and disease upon the Cross, so that we could righteously be freed from it.

The Bible says:

He Himself took our infirmities and bore our sicknesses. (Matthew 8:17).

Who Himself bore our sins in His own body on the tree, that we, having died to sins, might live for righteousness—by whose stripes you were healed. (1 Peter 2:24).

He sent His word [Jesus, the Word that became flesh, John 1] and healed them, and delivered them from their destructions. (Psalm 107:20).

…His visage [Jesus' appearance] was marred more than any man, and His form more than the sons of men. (Isaiah 52:14)

Do you see it? Jesus willfully died in our place, as our substitutional sacrifice and offering to the Father, to restore us to righteousness and to free us from the bondage of the Curse which includes, guilt, shame, sickness, disease, poverty, and so much more.

His sin ravaged body didn't even look human according to Isaiah 52:14, Sin made Him look like a grotesque piece of ripped flesh. Think of the effects of cancer, diabetes, gangrene, and every other sickness and disease mixed with the horrible scourging He received which lacerated and tore His body exposing His bones.

In Psalm 22, David speaks prophetically of Jesus, the Suffering Servant saying, "[16] For dogs [despicable and blood-thirsty people and demons] have surrounded Me; the congregation of the wicked has enclosed Me. They pierced My hands and My feet; [17] I can count all My bones. They [My bones] look and stare at Me."

In fact, Satan believed that he had won the battle against God by nailing Jesus to the Cross, but, Jesus offered Himself willingly otherwise they never would have been able to take Him and nail Him to the Cross. (See John 18:4-6).

The thing Satan didn't realize was that Jesus was innocent—He was perfect and sinless—and therefore, it was an illegal act to make an innocent man pay the penalty for a crime He didn't commit. That is how the Curse was reversed by Jesus.

Romans 6:23 says, "For the wages of sin is death, but the gift of God is eternal life in Christ Jesus our Lord." Jesus was sinless. The wages He deserved was LIFE, not death. But He humbled Himself to death to give us the life He deserved. Praise God!

I want you to know – EVERYTIME YOU PARTAKE OF COMMUNION, YOU ARE REVERSING THE CURSE IN YOUR BODY!

Jesus' Body was broken so that YOU could be HEALED! When you take the bread, YOU need to see YOUR sickness YOUR lack, YOUR whatever, on Jesus' body on that Cross. He died for YOU so that YOU could live. As you partake of it RELEASE YOUR FAITH FOR FORGIVENESS of sins and for HIS HEALING POWER to transfer to YOU.

The last misunderstanding that I want to correct is this: many pastors in the Church have taught that IF YOU have any sin in YOUR LIFE, YOU should abstain from partaking of The Lord's Supper/Communion or else YOU could die and become sick, because YOU are partaking "unworthily."

Nothing could be further from the truth! Jesus died for "sinners" and for "unworthy" people. We were once **_ALL_** sinners, but those of us who have received Jesus, are now redeemed saints, who still sin daily— even though we work (or do our best), to live righteous lives in Jesus. Praise God!

In 1 Corinthians 11:29-30 we read, "[29] For he who eats and drinks **_in an unworthy manner_** eats and drinks judgment to himself, **_not discerning the Lord's body. [30] For this reason many are weak and sick among you, and many sleep._**"

I want you to see something important here. Verse 30 says "For THIS REASON—SINGULAR—not for these reasons. Paul is saying that there is a singular reason that people are weak, sick and dead, and that is because they are partaking in an "UNWORTHY MANNER." Then he defines what that manner is: IT IS NOT "DISCERNING the LORD'S BODY."

In other words, Paul is saying that when we take communion and we do not understand that Jesus' body was broken and punished on the Cross—paying the debt for us to be made whole and free from the bondage of sickness and disease—we are taking the communion bread in an unworthy manner. Moreover, not recognizing what has been provided to us, is what leads to weakness, sickness, and even death.

Therefore, if we take His body (the Bread), in a worthy manner the opposite is true: 1. We will be strong, 2. We will be Healthy, and 3. We will remain alive and thriving.

You may be thinking to yourself, *"How can something as simple as eating a tiny piece of bread cause healing?"* Well my friend, it was the "simple" act of eating a piece of fruit in the Garden of Eden that caused the Fall.

Jesus has made every provision for YOUR health and wholeness through His death on the Cross. Decide today that you will begin to honor His sacrifice every time you take communion. If you have been given a bad report, take it three times a day just like you would medication. When you do, see your sickness transferred to His body and His healing transferred to yours. If you do this, you will reverse the Curse and allow His life-giving blood to set you free from sin, sickness, and death. Amen!

Daily Declaration

Thank You Father for the precious blood and body of Jesus! As I take communion today, I see myself whole because Jesus bore and suffered with sickness and disease on the Cross, so that I wouldn't have to. He shed His blood for the forgiveness of my sins. And I discern the Lord's body and I trade my sickness for His healing. I trade my unrighteousness for His righteousness. I trade my poverty for His wealth. I trade my depression for His joy. Everything that Jesus died to give to me, I receive by faith right Now in Jesus' name.

I declare that I am whole, healed, delivered, and blessed in Jesus' mighty name. As Isaiah 54:17 (AMP) states: "No weapon that is formed against me shall prosper, and every tongue that shall rise against me in judgment I shall show to be in the wrong. This [peace, righteousness, security, triumph over opposition] is the heritage of the servants of the Lord [those in whom the ideal Servant of the Lord is reproduced]; this is the righteousness or the vindication which I obtain from God [this is that which My Father imparts to me as my justification], says the Lord."

Healing is mine NOW! And nothing can change my mind. Not a negative report from the doctor, not pain, not anything! With LONG LIFE HE WILL SATISFY ME – In Jesus' Name! I have the victory TODAY, TOMORROW, AND EVERYDAY GOING FORWARD – in Jesus' name. AMEN!

Day 14
His Will Is PROSPERITY –Spirit, Soul, Body, & Materially

"Beloved, I wish above all things that thou mayest prosper and be in health, even as thy soul prospereth."

3 John 2 (KJV)

It is so clear from Scripture that God's will is always to see BLESSING in your life. Here in 3 John 2, John says, "ABOVE ALL ELSE..." In other words, what he is about to say is his highest desire for those who are hearing him. And as the mouthpiece of God, he can only say what the Father wills – otherwise he is not a good representative of his Father.

So, what was John's and the Father's highest desire? It was: 1. That you prosper: *euodoo*, literally, "to be led along a good road," "to complete an assigned task well," or "to succeed and be victorious." 2. And be in health: *hygiaino*, "to be sound," "to be whole and complete lacking nothing good," or "to have a well state of being in health as opposed to being sick." 3. Even as your soul prospers: *psyche euodoo*, meaning one's "inner self," "mind,' or "life breath," is "led along a good road," "completes its assigned task well," or "succeeds and is victorious."

That is powerful friends. John is telling us that God's will for our lives, is to be victorious in all that we do, living in perfect soundness and free from sickness and disease, lacking nothing good, even as our mind (which is the mind of Christ) and our inner being (our life breath [See Genesis 2:7], or spirit man) completes the task our Heavenly Father has sent us here to accomplish, in complete victory. AMEN!

Now that I have laid that foundation, look with me a Psalm 84:11 (AMP).

> For the Lord God is a Sun and Shield; the Lord bestows [present] grace and favor and [future] glory (honor, splendor, and heavenly bliss)! No good thing will He withhold from those who walk uprightly.

Let me ask you a question: What does the sun do? It shines its brilliance, glory, upon all creation and supplies the necessary light to provide nutrients through (photosynthesis) and everything else creation needs to thrive. Just as the Sun is the source of all good for nature, God is the Source of all things good for you and me.

Now what does a shield do for a soldier? It protects that soldier from the enemies' blows. Well Psalm 91 tell us that God is our refuge and great protector as well.

Psalm 84:11 also says that our Heavenly Father bestows GRACE and FAVOR upon us and WILL NOT withhold anything "GOOD" from us. Praise God! Is healing "GOOD?" YES! Is Prosperity 'GOOD?" YES! Is being able to provide for your family "GOOD?" YES, IT IS! Well then, I've got good news for you, God's not withholding those "GOOD THINGS" from YOU, Hallelujah!

In Psalm 34:10 (AMP) we find a similar promise:

> The young lions lack food and suffer hunger, but they who seek (inquire of and require) the Lord [by right of their need and on the authority of His Word], none of them shall lack any beneficial thing.

This passage may be a little confusing at first glance. Why would we care about "young lions" lacking food and suffering hunger, aren't lions, supposed to be the kings of the beasts and at the top of the food chain?

Well, after studying the words "young lions," I discovered that the words "young lions," could refer not only to literal lion whelps who can't hunt for themselves, but also to invading foreign armies that had no covenant with God (See Isaiah 5:26-29, Jeremiah 51:36-38).

In other words, God is speaking of non-covenant people—those who are outsiders to the privileges of covenant with Him. People like Goliath an "uncircumcised Philistine," according to David in 1 Samuel 17:26.

To paraphrase what David was saying, "Who does this NON-COVENANT yahoo think he is? I don't care how big and scary he looks, I know my God, and because I know Him and because He knows me through covenant—I CAN'T LOSE THIS BATTLE!

That's what Psalm 34:10 is referring to. It's those who don't have a covenant with God that are defeated. It's those who don't know their covenant rights and authority in Jesus that suffer. It's those outside of the commonwealth or citizenship of faith, that suffer hunger and lack.

Ephesians 2:11-13 (NLT) explains it this way:

> [11] Don't forget that you Gentiles used to be outsiders. You were called "uncircumcised heathens" by the Jews, who were proud of their circumcision, even though it affected only their bodies and not their hearts. [12] In those days you were living apart from Christ. You were excluded from citizenship among the people of Israel, and you did not know the covenant promises God had made to them. You lived in this world without God and without hope. [13] But now you have been united with Christ Jesus. Once you were far away from God, but now you have been brought near to him through the blood of Christ.

But the Bible promises that THOSE WHO "INQUIRE" [seek and ask of Him] and "REQUIRE" of the Lord [make a covenant faith demand, based on His covenant promises], by RIGHT OF THEIR NEED [as His covenant people], and on the AUTHORITY OF HIS WORD [based on His covenant promises], **SHALL NOT LACK ANY BENEFICIAL THING**. (Psalm 34:10, AMP)

Now that is truly GOOD NEWS my friend!

YOU and I as born-again believers in Jesus, have covenant rights and benefits, that unsaved people don't. We have the promise of spending eternity with Him in Heaven, the promise of peace, security, health and healing, protection, unearned and undeserved favor, prosperity, and so much more. Isn't it time we take hold of those promises NOW? AMEN.

Daily Declaration

Father, thank You for prospering me spirit, soul, body, and materially today. Jesus' work on the Cross was a perfect work, which restored me to righteousness and freed me from the Curse of sin, sickness, disease, fear, and poverty. I decree and declare that this TRUTH has made me FREE, in Jesus' mighty name.

John 8:32 promises, "And you shall know the truth, and the truth shall make you free."

Now that I know what Jesus has freed me from, I refuse to stay in bondage to those things. I present every covenant promise that You have made to me in the Bible, including but not limited to: Matthew 8:17, Isaiah 53:3-5, 1 Peter 2:24, and Psalm 107:20 as EXHIBIT A in my defense.

Moreover, I present Jesus, His sacrifice on the Cross and His standing as my High Priest, my Savior, and my Mediator of the New Covenant as EXHIBIT B, against the devil.

And Father, I ask You, that as the Just Judge of Heaven, that you will judge in my favor concerning these illegal symptoms that Satan has tried to make me submit to.

Jesus, will You please show Your stripes and the holes in Your wrists and in Your feet to the Father?

(Now, in your mind's eye, see the Father saying to you)

"I RULE IN FAVOR OF THE PLAINTIF—MY COVENANT CHILD! AND I DEMAND THAT HE/SHE BE LOOSED FROM ALL SYMPTOMS AND TRACES OF THE CURSE, THIS INSTANT – BASED ON THE EVIDENCE PROVIDED!"

(Now make this confession)

Healing, Wholeness, Perfect Soundness is mine right now, in Jesus' mighty name! I receive all that Jesus died to make available to me, NOW! AMEN!

Day 15
All Because Of The BLOOD

"But the blood on your houses will be a sign for your protection. When I see the blood, I will pass over you. Nothing will touch or destroy you..."

Exodus 12:13 (GWT)

I pray that you are beginning to understand the magnitude of God's love for YOU, as you are reading this devotional. God loves YOU so much and His desire is to see YOU well— WHOLE in every area of your life. That's because He created you for a specific purpose. He designed YOU for a particular mission that only YOU can fulfill. You are the only person on this earth that has the circle of influence that you have—YOU ARE SPECIAL— UNIQUE—and God wants to use YOU to influence and change the world.

In Exodus 12:13 we read about the original Passover which took place in Egypt. God had separated His people—the Hebrews, from the Egyptians by placing them in the land of Goshen. When He brought the plagues upon Egypt, because of Pharaoh's refusal to let God's people go, all of the Egyptians were affected by the plagues, but the Hebrews were not. Why is that? Because God was protecting His covenant people by separating them or creating a boundary or border around them—a hedge of protection.

We see an example of this hedge of protection in Job 1:10, "***Have You not made a hedge around him, [Job] around his household, and around all that he has on every side? You have blessed the work of his hands, and his possessions have increased in the land.***" (Emphasis Added).

What was going on in Job's life that would frustrate Satan, and make him complain about God protecting Job? Obviously, Satan had been trying to attack Job and trying to steal, kill, and destroy all that he had (See John 10:10), but he couldn't find a way to get at Job because he was a "Righteous man who hated evil" (See Job 1:1, 8). But what Satan hadn't realized was that Job had opened himself up to the devil through fear.

God wasn't saying, "Job is such a righteous man, now "sick'em devil" NO! God was just pointing out the fact that Job had opened himself up for attack through fear and unbelief.

Job had been operating in fear and unbelief, worrying about the safety of his children, because he didn't rest in the power of his covenant relationship with God. He misunderstood what it means to be righteousness, and instead of resting in righteousness, Job tried to "EARN" protection for his children, by offering multiple sacrifices (PLURAL).

That may not sound wrong when you first read it, but if Job had truly believed that God honors His covenant Word and that He would honor Job's sacrifice as an atonement or payment for his children's sin, he would have only offered one sacrifice and then rested in the knowledge that God is a just God! (See Job 1:4-5).

I've got news for you, if you have made Jesus the Lord of your life— You have been "MADE" the Righteousness of God in Jesus. (See 2 Corinthians 5:21). Hallelujah!!!

You're righteous whether you feel righteous or not. Even if you blew it and sinned two seconds ago, you are still RIGHTEOUS in God's eyes. So, quit allowing the enemy to remind you of your failures and just repent and move on declaring what God has already said about you. AMEN!

The Passover story is similar to the story of Job's sacrifice. Both are a prophetic symbol of the Messiah's role as our Passover Lamb (the full payment for our sin). In fact, in John 1:29 we read, "The next day John saw Jesus coming toward him, and said, "Behold! The Lamb of God who takes away the sin of the world!"

Jesus was and still is the only sacrifice that that frees us from the Curse of sin and its effects. His Blood cleanses us once and for all and keeps us out of the enemy's grasp.

Look at Exodus 12:13 (GWT), "But the blood on your houses will be a sign for your protection. When I see the blood, I will pass over you. ***NOTHING WILL TOUCH OR DESTROY YOU...***" (Emphasis Added).

The New Living Translation says, "...This ***PLAGUE OF DEATH*** will not touch you..." (Emphasis Added).

A word that is synonymous with plague is disease. God is saying that when He sees the BLOOD—No disease will be able to touch or destroy YOU! The question that I have for you is: Have you applied the BLOOD to your situation? Have you applied Jesus' BLOOD to the lentil (header) of your life? You may be a Christian. You may be saved and going to heaven, but that's not the same as applying the Blood to your life. The Hebrews were God's covenant people too, but they still had to apply the blood to the lentil (crossbeam of the door) and the door posts (the two sides), if they wanted to live through the night of the Passover.

You may be asking yourself, *How in the world do I do that?* I'm glad you asked. Revelation 12:11 (AMP) tells us, "And they have overcome (conquered) him [Satan] by means of the blood of the Lamb and by the utterance of their testimony..."

You can apply the BLOOD of Jesus by identifying with all that He has already done for you. By accepting the FINISHED WORK OF THE CROSS AS FULL PAYMENT FOR YOUR REDEMPTION AND HEALING!

His death paid for whatever you are going through right now. His BLOOD was poured out as an offering to free you from the bondage of sickness, disease, lack, confusion, and so much more.

The way we identify with Jesus' finished work is by meditating [muttering, speaking over and over], on Scriptures that tell us what He has done for us and seeing ourselves free, whole, and healed.

Let me give you an illustration of what I am saying. Let's take Psalm 91:3-7 (NLT) as an example. This passage says:

³ For he will rescue you from every trap and protect you from deadly disease. ⁴ He will cover you with his feathers. He will shelter you with his wings. *His faithful promises are your armor and protection.* ⁵ Do not be afraid of the terrors of the night, nor the arrow that flies in the day. *⁶ Do not dread the disease that stalks in darkness, nor the disaster that strikes at midday. ⁷ Though a thousand fall at your side, though ten thousand are dying around you, these evils will not touch you.* (Emphasis Added).

The first question you must ask yourself when you read a promise like this is: Do I really believe what is being said to me? Do I believe that God really means what He said here?

This may sound ridiculous at first, but let me make it easier for you to understand. Do you truly believe that God's Word can protect you from EVERY form of harm and evil? From cancer, from Ebola, from a nuclear blast, God forbid, if it should happen in your neighborhood?

I DO! I believe that no matter what happens around me, God has set-up a hedge of protection—an invisible border, just like He set-up between Egypt and Goshen, where death and destruction cannot enter in and harm me or my family.

I believe that even if a nuclear bomb exploded feet in front of me, somehow, I would be covered by God's wings—in the Secret Place of the Most High, and no harm would come near me. A thousand people may fall dead on one side of me and ten thousand on the other side, but God would protect me from it all.

If you want to enjoy the healing, the protection, the Blessing that the Bible promises for every covenant child of God, you must make the Bible your FINAL AUTHORITY. You must have the attitude that: if the Bible says it, I believe it, and that settles it—no matter how crazy or beyond reason it may sound.

When the enemy brings an attack your way, pull out your sword (your Bible) and declare, "Devil, I bind you in the name of Jesus! No weapon formed against me will prosper (Isaiah 54:17). I have been redeemed from the curse through Jesus' death (Galatians 3:13-14). Jesus bore every sickness, every disease, all poverty and lack, so that I don't have to (Isaiah 53:3-5, Matthew 8:17, 2 Peter 2:24).

I refuse to accept anything that Jesus has already paid for and anything that I have been redeemed from. The curse has no part in me because I belong to Jesus (Galatians 3:29, Deuteronomy 28:1-14). I am the healed of the Lord and I walk in soundness, wholeness, prosperity, and perfect healing in Jesus' mighty name!

I apply the BLOOD of Jesus to my life and I testify to its power working in me now and continuously making me whole. (Revelation 12:11). GO NOW! Peddle your trash somewhere else. I resist you and you must flee in Jesus' name, AMEN! (1 Peter 5:6-9).

Daily Declaration

Thank You Father for your protection over me and my family. I plead the precious Blood of Jesus over us, as a covering and hedge of protection. I declare that LIFE and SUPERNATURAL FAVOR go before us and behind us as a shield keeping us out of harm's way. (See Psalms 5:12).

I declare that every weapon that is formed against me and my loved ones is destroyed from the onset in Jesus' name! (Isaiah 54:17). Though trials may come, the Bible promises me that I will ALWAYS be victorious IN JESUS (See 1 Corinthians 15:57 and 2 Corinthians 2:14).

Father, help me to guard my mouth and to speak faith instead of doubt and fear. I know how powerful my words are, and I purpose to speak life and faith and to glorify You in all that I do and say. Just like the Apostle Paul said:

> [13-15] We're not keeping this quiet, not on your life. Just like the psalmist who wrote, "I believed it, so I said it," we say what we believe. And what we believe is that the One who raised up the Master Jesus will just as certainly raise us up with you, alive. Every detail works to your advantage and to God's glory: more and more grace, more and more people, more and more praise! [16-18] So we're not giving up. How could we! Even though on the outside it often looks like things are falling apart on us, on the inside, where God is making new life, not a day goes by without his unfolding grace. These hard times are small potatoes compared to the coming good times, the lavish celebration prepared for us. There's far more here than meets the eye. The things we see now are here today, gone tomorrow. But the things we can't see now will last forever.

I love the Amplified Bible's rendering of verse 18: "Since we consider and look not to the things that are seen but to the things that are unseen; for the things that are visible are temporal (brief and fleeting), but the things that are invisible are deathless and everlasting." I AM and OVERCOMMER! I AM HEALED, in Jesus, AMEN!

Day 16
The God Who Gives Life To The
Dead & Changes Circumstances

"(As it is written, I have made thee a father of many nations,) before him whom he believed, even God, who quickeneth the dead, and calleth those things which be not as though they were."

Romans 4:17 (KJV)

Years ago while I was attending Oral Roberts University, I was faced with a situation that seemed impossible at the time, to overcome. I had left a successful career in medical sales to pursue ministry, and what I believed, God had ordained for my life. As a result, I was no longer making a six-figure income, but my financial responsibilities had not changed much—I still had large monthly bills that needed to be paid.

Patty, my wife and I had recently moved to Tulsa Oklahoma and purchased a new home. God had favored us tremendously with the bountiful sale of our home in California. We purchased our new home in Tulsa, thinking that our careers in Tulsa, would pay similar to what we had earned in California, but we were wrong.

About eight months into our new mortgage, I realized I was in trouble. I had gone back to waiting tables at a local five-star steak house, but was making only a third of the salary I would have made back in California. And I soon found myself falling behind on all of my bills.

Trying to remedy the situation, I soon picked up three morning paper routes, which I worked from my car—a Mercedes SUV. Sure, it wasn't very practical to dirty up the inside with ink from the news print, or to put all the extra miles on our only vehicle, but we didn't have any other choice at the time—or so we thought.

Even with my waiting position at the steak house and my three paper routes, I was still not making what I needed to pay all of our bills. Patty soon got a job as the Children's Ministry Director at the church we attended, but we were still struggling to make ends meet.

Exhausted from my crazy schedule and desperate for help, I cried out to God at two o'clock each morning while throwing papers and begged Him for breakthrough.

On the third morning while at school, a friend of mine came up to me and said, "Mike, the Lord has told me to pay your mortgage this month. If you'll allow me, I'd love to sow a seed and pay your house payment."

I was thrilled, but pride was trying to raise its ugly head. This young man was ten years younger than me. He had a wife and child of his own to care for, and I didn't want Him or anyone else knowing my business or to think that I needed help—I was a "MAN OF FAITH" after all.

I desperately wanted the gift, but I almost allowed my pride to steal God's blessing by brushing him off and saying something like, "Thanks brother, but really, I'm ok."

Thank God, my friend knew he had heard from Heaven and was persistent about being obedient. He looked me straight in the eyes and said, "Mike, you aren't going to steal my blessing. God told me to sow this seed and I'm going to sow it whether you like it or not. How much is your mortgage?" I told him, and received the gift joyfully.

A couple of days later, a lady friend of mine who was living in California called early in the morning while I was throwing papers saying that the Lord had awakened her and instructed her to send $3000.00 to me, specifically for my mortgage. I received the gift and thanked her for her generosity and obedience.

Within just a couple of days I had miraculously gone from utter fear of losing my home and living on the streets to having more than enough to pay my mortgage for the next three months. God had come through

BIG TIME! He not only answered my prayer for my immediate needs, but for my future need as well. Hallelujah!

This story reminds me of Romans 4:17 and God's ability to give life to dead things. The word "quicken" in verse 17, is the Greek word *zoopoieo*, which is a compound derived from two words *zoon* and *poieo*. Together the words mean "to make alive" to "give life to" or "to vitalize."

God had answered my prayer and changed my circumstances from being "dead" [no hope], and brought them back to life. I had gotten myself into this mess on my own, by failing to research and plan properly before purchasing my new home. But God had breathed resurrection life back into my finances by sending two separate people to sow blessing into me.

The word "dead," in this passage, is the Greek word *nekros*, which means to be "dead," "lifeless," or "useless." In the New Testament, *nekros* often refers to lifeless bodies that are either buried or "fit to be buried."

If you can grab ahold of what I'm about to say, I believe it will change your life forever. Romans 4:17 is literally telling us that no matter how dead or lifeless our situations may seem, GOD CAN AND WILL, TAKE WHAT IS DEAD AND BREATHE RESSURECTION LIFE BACK INTO THEM, IF YOU WILL BELIEVE HIM!

He did it with Abraham and Sarah. She went from being barren to giving birth to Isaac. He did it with Isaac who was slated to be an offering upon Mt. Moriah, but God provided the ram in the thicket. He did it with Hannah who had been barren, but later gave birth to the prophet Samuel, He did it with David, who was being hunted down by King Saul, but ended up becoming King of Israel himself. And He'll do it for you too.

When I look back over all the times God has performed miracles in my life, some of them seem so minor to my rational mind, but they were ALL HUGE at the time. During this particular period, while attending ORU, I had given up everything I had to follow God. Most of my friends and almost all of our family thought we were nuts and that we had joined a cult and fallen off the deep end.

But let me remind you of a certainty. If you don't get anything else out of this devotional, please understand this: No matter what you are facing—no matter how impossible your situation looks—WITH GOD, ALL THINGS ARE POSSIBLE! (See Matthew 19:23-30, Mark 9:23, Mark 10:27, Luke 1:37).

NOTHING IS TOO DIFFICULT FOR GOD! (See Genesis 18:14, Job 42:2, Jeremiah 32:27, Luke 18:27, Hebrews 6:18).

I dare you to believe God for your immediate healing, wholeness, restoration, and prosperity. Whatever you are facing, HE IS ABLE! He is the God who calls those things which be not as though they were. In other words, He resurrects the dead things we give to Him and breathes His divine life back into them! Praise God! He Is Good!!!

Daily Declaration

Father, thank You for breathing life into my body, into my spirit, into my finances, into my career, into my marriage, into my relationships, into every facet of my life—in Jesus' name!

With You Lord Jesus, NOTHING is impossible! You are a friend who sticks closer than a brother and cares for even "the small challenges" I face each day. Nothing that I struggle with is "too small or inconvenient" for Your concern. You love me with a red hot passionate love and I am grateful for You and love You too Lord.

Father, You said in James 4:2, that we don't have what we want because we don't ask You for it.

It's pride that often gets in my way of seeing Your best in my life—and I repent of it now, in Jesus' name. Forgive me Father for believing the lies of the enemy. Forgive me for doubting Your love for me. Forgive me for thinking that anything that I need, or desire is "insignificant" in Your eyes. And forgive me for trying to be my own source, when You have promised to be my God and my Source in ALL THINGS. (Leviticus 26:45; Philippians 4:19; Hebrews 10:8; Revelation 21:7).

So, today, as an act of my faith, I ask You for these things in the mighty name of Jesus!

Physical Needs:

Emotional Needs:

Spiritual Needs:

Material Needs:

Relational Needs:

I receive them all NOW, in Jesus' name, AMEN!

Day 17
The Word Is Working Mightily In Me

"*20* My son, give attention to my words; incline your ear to my sayings. *21* Do not let them depart from your eyes; keep them in the midst of your heart; *22* For they are life to those who find them, and health to all their flesh."

(Proverbs 4:20-22)

God's Word—The Bible is medicine, but only to those who will hear His promises continuously, because faith comes by hearing (Romans 10:17), and for those who will speak them continuously, because life and death are in the power of the tongue (Proverbs 18:20-21). For this group of people, God says they are life and health to ALL THEIR FLESH.

When we look closer into the literal meaning of the words or phrases of Proverbs 4:20-22 we uncover some amazing hidden truths. The words: "give attention to," is from the Hebrew word: *qashab*, which means "to pay attention to" or "to listen carefully to what is being said."

The phrase "incline your ear," is from the Hebrew words: *natah attah ozen*, which means "to bend toward carefully," or "to bend towards revelation, or towards something that is being revealed."

David's words, "keep them in the midst of your heart," in Hebrew: *shamar hemmah tavek attah lebab*, literaly means to, "diligently guard those things revealed internally through purposeful thought and consideration."

And the words: "For they are life to those who find them, and health to all their flesh," *ki hemmah chay matsa hemmah marpe kol hi basar*, means: "certainly they are living and flowing with life and are a healing cure to the person who will seek after them."

That is powerful my friends, The Lord has promised that if we will listen carefully to what He is revealing to us, and bend our way of believing toward His healing promises in Scripture, diligently guarding those powerful truths through purposeful meditation and declaration, they will certainly cause us to flow with life and they will manifest a healing cure to every cell, tissue, organ, bone, and fiber in our bodies.

This revelation sheds a broader light upon Psalm 103:5 where the psalmist declares, "Bless the Lord…Who satisfies your mouth with good things, so that your youth is renewed like the eagle's."

In other words, when we meditate upon (chew on and mutter), the promises of the Bible, they not only change us in a spiritual way, but those healing promises change our physical DNA too. What was once old and decaying because we live in a fallen and sin infected world, has become new, fresh, and flowing with the life of God.

There are many more Scriptures throughout the Bible that teach this same principle, but I want to focus on one more passage today. In Proverbs 3 we read:

> [1]My son, do not forget my law [Torah = teaching, instructions, covenant Word], but let your heart keep my commands [commandments, terms or prescriptions]; [2] ***For length of days and long life and peace they will add to you.*** [3] Let not mercy and truth forsake you; bind them around your neck, write them on the tablet of your heart, [4] And so find favor and high esteem in the sight of God and man. [5] Trust in the LORD with all your heart, and lean not on your own understanding; [6] In all your ways acknowledge Him, and He shall direct your paths. [7] ***Do not be wise in your own eyes; fear the LORD and depart from evil.*** [8] ***It will be health to your flesh, and strength to your bones…*** [13] Happy is the man who finds wisdom, and the man

who gains understanding; [14] For her proceeds are better than the profits of silver, and her gain than fine gold. [15] She is more precious than rubies, and all the things you may desire cannot compare with her. *[16] Length of days is in her right hand, in her left-hand riches and honor. [17] Her ways are ways of pleasantness, and all her paths are peace. [18] She is a tree of life to those who take hold of her, and happy are all who retain her...* [21] My son, let them not depart from your eyes— keep sound wisdom and discretion; *[22] So they will be life to your soul and grace to your neck. [23] Then you will walk safely in your way, and your foot will not stumble. [24] When you lie down, you will not be afraid; yes, you will lie down and your sleep will be sweet.* (Proverbs 3:1-8, 13-18, 21-24, Emphasis Added).

God's Word – His precious promises, have life and power flowing through them. When we read the Bible, it's important that we not only read, but that we feed upon what is being said to us. The Bible is not meant for us to just to read passively and then walk away, checking off a box on our daily "to do list." No! God's Word is life-giving, healing power, that is meant to be infused into our entire person – spirit, soul, and body – and meant to renew, refresh, and revitalize us from the top of our heads to the soles of our feet – inside and out.

I love the way Paul explained it to the Thessalonians, "Therefore, we never stop thanking God that when you received His message from us, you didn't think of our words as mere human ideas. You accepted what we said as the very Word of God—which, of course, it is. And this Word continues to work in you who believe. (1 Thessalonians 2:13, NLT).

God's Word is like dynamite! It has the explosive ability to heal, renew, deliver, and breathe life into the dead and decaying things in our lives. If received by faith and put to work through meditation and confession, His promise will impart life, health, and vibrancy – transforming the very nature and circumstances we face, and make impossibilities, possible! Hallelujah!

I am so grateful that God's Word works continuously in me. It never takes a break! It never stalls out, based on my performance of good works or sin. And it always leads me to perfect health and wholeness in Christ Jesus! Amen.

His Word is working mightily in me because I believe it, I speak it, I chew on it by meditating on it, and I allow it to transform me from the inside out—renewing my youth as the eagles—in Jesus' mighty name! Amen!

Daily Declaration

I praise You Father, for Your goodness, Your favor, and Your Word, which is always working mightily in me, in Jesus' name. Thank You for Jesus, my Lord and Savior, who died to give me perfect health and freedom from every symptom of the Curse.

Galatians 3:13-14 says, "[13] Christ has redeemed us from the curse of the law, having become a curse for us…[14] that the blessing of Abraham might come upon the Gentiles [the non-Jews, the nations of the world] in Christ Jesus, that we might receive the promise of the Spirit through faith."

If He became the Curse, in my place (for my sins), then I will honor Him by becoming perfectly sound – spirit, soul, and body, just as He was and is. Sin could not stick to Him because there was no sin in Him or on Him. He was and is immune to the Curse.

In fact, the only way He could die on the Cross was by faith. He became my sin by faith! Therefore, I walk in His perfect health by faith! I believe that I have perfect soundness now in Jesus' name!

"He Himself took my infirmities and bore my sicknesses." (Matthew 8:17).

Jesus "bore my sins in His own body on the tree, that I, having died to sins, might live for righteousness—by whose stripes **I AM HEALED!** (1 Peter 2:24, Emphasis Added).

I declare that, "Jesus, the Living Word who became flesh (John 1:14), my Lord and Savior, became the righteous and just payment for my sins (John 3:16). His divine power is working mightily in me to eradicate everything that is not in line with the Blessing.

Sickness, death, and disease, you have no legal right to operate in my body! Jesus defeated you! I resist you now, and you must flee in Jesus' name! (James 4:7). I plead His precious blood over myself today, and I declare myself off limits to sin, sickness, and death!

Life flows through me in abundance. Health and healing are mine to enjoy! I will live and not die, and I will declare the faithful works of the Lord – who is my refuge, my strength, and a very present help in my time of Trouble. I REFUSE TO FEAR in Jesus' mighty name, AMEN! (See Psalm 118:17, Psalm 46:1-2).

Day 18
Your Faith Will Change Your Circumstances

"While we do not look at the things which are seen, but at the things which are not seen. For the things which are seen are temporary, but the things which are not seen are eternal."

2 Corinthians 4:18

I find it interesting that while those in the world often declare, that seeing is believing, God's Word declares the exact opposite. It is amazing that, so many people have been duped into believing the lies of the enemy, and so easily accept his deceptive tactics to steal, kill, and destroy their lives, even though Jesus told us that Satan is a liar – and the Father of all lies.

In John 8:44 (AMP), Jesus speaking to the Pharisees says, "You are of your father, the devil, and it is your will to practice the lusts and gratify the desires [which are characteristic] of your father. He was a murderer from the beginning and does not stand in the truth, because there is no truth in him. When he speaks a falsehood, he speaks what is natural to him, for he is a liar [himself] and the father of lies and of all that is false."

I say all this to make the point that Satan never speaks a complete truth. He is crafty and sly, and he twists the truth in the attempt to deceive and destroy. In fact, he will often take a partial truth from Scripture and then twist it, so that those hearing him will think they are hearing God's Word when in fact, they are being lied to.

In Genesis 3:1 we read, "Now the serpent was more cunning than any beast of the field which the LORD God had made. And he said to the woman, "Has God indeed said, 'You shall not eat of every tree of the garden'?"

Satan's objective here was to cause Eve to doubt the goodness of God and thereby drive a wedge of fear between her and her Father. He was trying to convince her to believe that God was keeping something "good" and "beneficial" away from her.

In Ephesians 6:11 the Apostle Paul warns believers to, "Put on the whole armor of God, that you may be able to stand against ***the wiles of the devil.***"

The word "wiles" is translated from the Greek word *methodeias*, which is the act of craftily scheming with the intent to deceive or to bewitch another.

The word "bewitch" is an interesting word itself, because bewitching is the act of using "black magic" or "dark arts" to deceive. So, in other words, there are spiritual powers of deception at work when someone is being bewitched—powers that aren't necessarily obvious to the human eye or perception.

That is why Paul exhorts us to be strong in the Lord and in the power of **HIS MIGHT**, by putting on:

> [11] ...the whole armor of God, that you may be able to stand against the wiles of the devil. [12] For we do not wrestle against flesh and blood, but against principalities, against powers, against the rulers of the darkness of this age, against spiritual hosts of wickedness in the heavenly places. [13] Therefore take up the whole armor of God, that you may be able to withstand in the evil day, and having done all, to stand. [14] Stand therefore, having girded your waist with truth, having put on the breastplate of righteousness, [15] and having shod your feet with the preparation of the gospel of peace; [16] above all, taking the shield of faith with which you will be able to quench all the fiery darts of the wicked one. [17] And take the helmet of salvation, and the sword of the Spirit, which is the word of God; [18] praying always with all prayer

and supplication in the Spirit, being watchful to this end with all perseverance and supplication for all the saints

In fact, when Paul writes to the Galatians he says, "O foolish Galatians! **_Who has <u>bewitched</u> you that you should not obey the truth_**, before whose eyes Jesus Christ was clearly portrayed among you as crucified?" (Galatians 3:1).

To put in in today's vernacular, Paul is asking the Galatians, "Have you been outsmarted again by that lying devil? Are you that dim-witted, that you can't see his deceiving fingerprints all over what's going on here? You've been taught THE TRUTH, but you have fallen for THE LIE again."

However, Paul might as well be asking us the same question. I say this because we fall for the same spiritual deceptions, the same lies, the same smoke and mirrors, that the devil has been using to deceive and defeat people for countless millennia.

For example, let's say we go to the doctor, run some tests, and are told that we have some "incurable" disease or condition. Many of us accept the doctor's report as "THE GOSPEL," as the truth and the highest authority concerning the matter. And, why shouldn't we? After all, he or she is an "expert" in the field of medicine. Many of these doctors have spent decades caring for patients and helping them alleviate symptoms and reduce pain.

Please don't misunderstand me when I say this, but the doctor's word isn't SUPREME AUTHORITY. The doctor's word will never trump GOD'S WORD, unless we believe the doctor's word over God's! In fact, whichever word we elevate and magnify as THE TRUTH will be what we will have in life. God made this crystal clear in Proverbs 18:20-21 and Proverbs 23:7.

Don't misunderstand me. God gave us doctors to help us with "natural," "earthly" methods of healing, but when doctors fail and have nothing left they can do—*Jehovah Rapha* is still able!

NOTHING IS TOO DIFFICULT FOR ALMIGHTY GOD—HE SPECIALIZES IN THE IMPOSSIBLE! (See Genesis 18:14, Jeremiah 32:17, 27, and Luke 18:27).

Over and over throughout the Bible, we are reminded how God honors the faith of those who will believe Him for their miracle. He continually honors those who dare to believe His precious promises over what they see, hear, feel, taste and touch in this natural realm.

Our Father Abraham, is an example of this Biblical truth. He and Sarah faced infertility, but God gave them a son as promised. He faced death and loss, but God brought deliverance. He was even asked to sacrifice Isaac, but Abraham understood the power of a covenant promise. He knew that if God asked him to offer up Isaac as a sacrifice, the only way God could fulfill His promise, was to raise Isaac back up from the dead.

The Bible says, "Abraham believed God, and it was credited to him as righteousness." (See Genesis 15:6, Romans 4:3, Galatians 3:6, James 2:23).

We find this same SPIRIT OF FAITH that Abraham typified in David. In Psalm 116 we read:

> [1] I love the LORD because he hears my voice and my prayer for mercy. [2] Because he bends down to listen, I will pray as long as I have breath! [3] Death wrapped its ropes around me; the terrors of the grave overtook me. I saw only trouble and sorrow. [4] Then I called on the name of the LORD: "Please, LORD, save me!" [5] How kind the LORD is! How good he is! So merciful, this God of ours! [6] The LORD protects those of childlike faith; I was facing death, and he saved me. [7] Let my soul be at rest again, for the LORD has been good to me. [8] He has saved me from death, my eyes from tears, my feet from stumbling. [9] And so I walk in the LORD's presence as I live here on earth! [10] ***I believed in you, so I said***, "I am deeply troubled, LORD." [11] In my anxiety I cried out to you, "These people are all liars!" [12] What can I offer the LORD for all he has done for me? [13] I will lift up the cup of salvation and praise

the LORD's name for saving me. (Psalm 116:1-13, NLT, Emphasis Added).

You really need to pay attention to verse 10 of Psalm 116. David says that because he believed the Lord...it caused him to speak...What was it that David both believed and spoke? David obviously believed in God's goodness. He believed in God's love for Him. He believed God's promises to care for him and to be his covenant Father, who would protect him in trouble, deliver him from his enemies, and heal him from any plague that would try to kill him.

You might be thinking to yourself, *how do you know this Mike?* I know it because David wrote about these things is Psalm 23, Psalm 91, Psalm 103, and even Psalm 116.

We have the evidence—the PROOF available to us in David's own words. In fact, David's faith in God, is unmistakable. He believed God! He trusted God to see him through every "IMPOSSIBLE" situation he encountered. And God was ***ALWAYS FAITHFUL!***

We could easily say the same of David that God said of Abraham, ***David believed God and it was accounted to him as righteousness.*** In fact, God called David a man after His own heart! Why? Because even in the midst of chaos, in the midst of impending death, David always chose to trust his Heavenly Father over what he could see with his own two eyes.

David knew his Father's character. He trusted in God's unfailing love, even though he struggled with sin and failed at obeying God perfectly. David still believed that God would be rich in grace and mercy and that He would fulfill His promises, even though David didn't deserve His mercy. That is powerful folks—that is truly **AMAZING GRACE!**

In 2 Corinthians 4:13 Paul reminds us of Abraham's and David's bold faith. In fact, 2 Corinthians 4:13 is Paul's attempt to teach us the Biblical principle that David put into operation in Psalm 116:10 when He said, "I believe and therefore I spoke..."

And since we have the same spirit of faith, according to what is written, "I believed and therefore I spoke," we also believe and therefore speak. (2 Corinthians 4:13).

Just as Paul encourages us to be imitators of God since we are His covenant children (See Ephesians 5:1), he also encourages us to have the same spirit of faith that both Abraham and David had when they believed God and spoke God's promises to themselves every time they faced negative situations.

Speaking God's promises, reminding ourselves of His mercy, and grace, are ways of building ourselves up for the battle we're fighting. In fact, in Revelation 12:11 we read, "And they overcame him by the blood of the Lamb and by the word of their testimony, and they did not love their lives to the death."

What you say about your situation is more important than what the doctor has said about it. When you align your words and your faith with God's Word—YOU CAN'T LOSE!

In 2 Corinthians 4:13, Paul is trying to teach us that what we believe from the Word, has the power to change our natural circumstances and to over-ride the power of darkness. Jesus' death, His blood, and His name are more powerful than every obstacle we face. Jesus overcame death, hell, and the grave and so have we—IN HIM—Hallelujah!

Paul concludes by exhorting us to dismiss what we "see" in the natural. We must remember that the enemy uses dark and lying supernatural power, in the attempt to deceive and bewitch us into believing his lies. He will even try to use lying symptoms that manifest in our bodies as evidence that our faith in God is not working. But if we will dare to believe and to speak God's Word—God immediately counts our faith as righteousness, and goes to work driving out disease and healing everything that needs healing.

Paul writes:

> So, we're not giving up. How could we! Even though on the outside it often looks like things are falling apart on us, on the inside, where God is making new life, not a day goes by without his unfolding grace. These hard times are small potatoes compared to the coming good times, the lavish celebration prepared for us. There's far more here than meets the eye. The things we see now are here today, gone tomorrow. But the things we can't see now will last forever. (2 Corinthians 4:16-18, MSG).

I love the Amplified Bible's rendering of 2 Corinthians 4:18, "Since we consider and look not to the things that are seen but to the things that are unseen; for the things that are visible are temporal (brief and fleeting), but the things that are invisible are deathless and everlasting."

In other words, since we don't allow anything but God's Word to be the FINAL AUTHORITY in our lives, Satan has no choice but to run away in defeat.

Hallelujah! Our Heavenly Father's covenant promises will ALWAYS prevail in our lives—if we will believe them and speak them, even in the midst of the negative circumstances we face.

Daily Declaration

Father, today, I thank You for Your covenant Word which has the power to over-ride, rearrange, and to change, every situation and every circumstance that I face.

There is nothing as stable, true, and constant as Your Holy Word. I decree and declare that Your promises in the Bible are what I have determined to be the STANDARD for my life and the lives of my family members.

In the mighty name of Jesus, I declare myself whole and lacking no good thing according to Psalm 34:10-18 and Psalm84:11 and James 1:4.

Holy Spirit, I ask you to put a guard over my mouth. Whenever I am tempted to say something negative or contrary to my Father's Word, help me to catch myself and to speak the Word only.

I curse every negative thing that I have spoken over myself and command it to be broken off and to become unfruitful this instant, in Jesus' name.

I command life, perfect health, and peace to come upon me NOW, in Jesus' name. Lord Jesus, You said that You would never leave me or forsake me. Therefore, I ask You to heal and to transform every cell, tissue, bone, organ and fiber, that needs healing. I reach out to You by faith, and take hold of my healing this instant, in Jesus' name. Amen!

(Now, if you believe that you have received your healing, do something you couldn't do earlier—and then give Jesus your praise).

Day 19
Faith Is Your Title Deed

"Now faith is the assurance (the confirmation, the title deed) of the things [we] hope for, being the proof of things [we] do not see and the conviction of their reality [faith perceiving as real fact what is not revealed to the senses]."

Hebrews 11:1 (AMP)

In yesterday's study, we discovered that what we see isn't always what will be. Circumstances don't have to last, they are temporary and changeable. This is especially true when we put our faith to work, taking hold of God's precious promises, and believing Him to do exactly what He has promised in the Bible.

People often say, *but Mike, how are you so certain that it will turn out the way that you think it will?* To which I can confidently answer, "It's not what I think will happen—it's what I know will happen!

The Bible gives us proof that we can count on. Let me illustrate what I mean.

In Numbers 23:19 (ERV) we are told, "God is not a man; He will not lie. God is not a human being; His decisions will not change. If He says he will do something, then He will do it. If He makes a promise, then He will do what he promised."

We are also told, "My word, which comes from my mouth, is like the rain and snow. It will not come back to me without results. It will accomplish whatever I want and achieve whatever I send it to do." (Isaiah 55:11, GWT).

You don't ever have to question whether your Heavenly Father **wants** you to be healed, whole, prosperous or to walk in every other part of the Blessing. He has shown us over and over that healing *IS* His will.

All you need to do, is to study Scriptures like (Psalm 107:20; Psalm 121:7-8, Matthew 4:23-24, Matthew 8:17, Luke 6:19, 1 Peter 2:24, 3 John 2), and you'll know for certain too.

So, when you read Scriptures like the one above (Isaiah 55:11, GWT) that talk about God doing what He "**wants**," find out what the Bible says regarding your situation. Then, find yourself two or three Scriptural witnesses which prove God's will for your healing, prosperity, etc., and begin renewing your mind to those promises.

The Bible says repeatedly, "By the mouth of two or three witnesses every word shall be established." (2 Corinthians 13:1).

It's not enough to think you know about a promise located somewhere in the Bible or to sort of know a Scripture that your pastor taught on, when you're in the heat of a battle. YOU'VE GOT TO HAVE PROOF! YOU MUST HAVE IRREFUTEABLE EVIDENCE, in order to overcome your adversary! We don't always have the convenience of time to search for promises when the devil's breathing down our necks, when he's trying to steamroll our faith, and attempting to take our life—it may be too late by then.

No! When the devil comes in like a flood trying to steal the Word and your confidence in whatever you are believing God for, you need to be ready to say, NO DEVIL! IT IS WRITTEN…

Jesus told us about the devil's tactics in Mark chapter 4 and in Matthew 13 saying, "[18] Therefore hear the parable of the sower: [19] ***When anyone hears the word of the kingdom, and does not understand it, then the wicked one comes and snatches away what was sown in his heart.*** This is he who received seed by the wayside. [20] *But he who received the seed on stony places, this is he who hears the word and immediately receives it with joy; [21] yet he has no root in himself, but endures only for a while. **For when tribulation or persecution arises because of the word, immediately he stumbles.**"* (Matthew 13:18-19).

Do you see that? Satan always comes trying to steal the Word—God's promises—through confusion or by helping you to misunderstand the TRUTH. An example of this is when he tries to make you believe that everything the Bible teaches is only "SPIRITUAL" in nature.

For example, in 2 Corinthians 8:9 we read, "For you know the grace of our Lord Jesus Christ, that though He was rich, yet for your sakes He became poor, that you through His poverty might become rich."

The devil and even some well-meaning pastors who are ignorant of Biblical truth and living by personal experience rather than making the Word of God their FINAL AUTHORITY, might tell you, "Paul was talking about us becoming "Spiritually rich," because Jesus became "spiritually poor." Paul wasn't talking about us becoming rich in material things.

But if you think about this for even a second, you could prove the devil and these people wrong. Just ask yourself this question: How could a spiritually poor Jesus, heal the sick, raise the dead, and perform all the amazing miracles He performed, if He was "spiritually poor?" He couldn't—plain and simple!

God doesn't have a problem with people being rich and blessed in every area of life, otherwise He would need to repent to Abraham, Solomon, Job, and a whole host of other people in the Bible.

In fact, in Genesis 13:2, the Bible says, "Abram was ***VERY RICH*** in ***LIVESTOCK***, in ***SILVER***, and in ***GOLD***." (Emphasis Added). You're NEVER going to convince me that cattle, gold, and silver is referring to "SPIRITUAL" things. NO, PLEASE! Let the elevator go to the top! Those things are most definitely PROOF of Abraham's MATERIAL WEALTH.

In John 10:10 (AMP) Jesus calls Satan THE THIEF, and He tells us about his character as opposed to Jesus' character saying: "***The thief comes only in order to steal and kill and destroy.*** I came that they may have and enjoy life, and have it in abundance (to the full, till it overflows)."

The best way to make sure that you are never cheated out of the things that rightfully belong to you as a child of God and joint-heir with Jesus (Romans 8:16-17), is to:

1. Pray and ask the Father to reveal His will concerning your situation and circumstances.

2. Find out what the Bible says concerning that area and find a minimum of two or three witnesses from Scripture to provide supporting evidence for whatever it is you need or desire.

3. Once you have your evidence from the Bible – renew your mind to the truth of God's promises.

4. And feed your faith daily by meditating on and speaking those Scriptures over your situation until you experience your breakthrough.

5. And finally, NEVER GIVE UP! God's Word won't ever return void! (Isaiah 55:11).

I know you read it at the beginning of today's devotional, but always remember this undeniable truth:

Now faith is the assurance (the confirmation, the title deed) of the things [we] hope for, being the proof of things [we] do not see and the conviction of their reality [faith perceiving as real fact what is not revealed to the senses]. (Hebrews 11:1, AMP).

Your faith in God's promises, is your title deed to the things you are believing Him for. When the devil comes your way trying to cheat you out of what rightfully belongs to you, pull out your Scriptures, and read him the riot act.

Let him know that you have all the proof you need to support your stand of faith. Tell him that he might as well pack-up camp and get a move on—taking his lying symptoms and trash talk with him, because you know the TRUTH concerning your health, prosperity, marriage, etc. Then do what Jesus did when He was tempted by the devil in the wilderness. Declare—DEVIL, IT IS WRITTEN... And continue confessing your Scriptures out loud continually, until you've built up your faith, run him out of town, and are walking in your victory. Amen!

Daily Declaration

Father, I take hold of my title deed to healing, joy, provision, blessing, peace, and everything else Jesus gave His life to provide for me. I receive the fullness of the BLESSING of Abraham through My Lord and Savior Jesus.

Galatians 3:29 declares, "And if you are Christ's, then you are Abraham's seed, and heirs according to the promise." I am Christ's and He is mine. I am a joint-heir with Him according to Romans 8:16-17, sharing in every good thing that belongs to Him. I take hold of it all now, through faith, representing ALL that Jesus is and ALL that His blood has paid for. I receive my full inheritance NOW—in Jesus mighty name.

Thank You Jesus for dying for me. Thank You for taking everything that was wrong with me and making it right and reversing the Curse. Thank You Lord, for turning my mourning into dancing and my shame into righteousness. I am the righteousness of God in Christ Jesus! Hallelujah.

Lord, use me as a testimony for others. Let me bring glory and praise to Your name! Today, I shout for joy and declare my victory over sin, sickness, and death, in Jesus' mighty name. He took my penalty for sin and I take His reward, His perfect soundness—nothing missing, and nothing broken in my life—for His righteousness. I do this all by faith in Jesus—knowing that my redeemer lives! Amen and Amen.

Day 20
I AM The Lord Who Heals You!

"I will not make you suffer any of the diseases I sent on the Egyptians; for I am the LORD who heals you."

Exodus 15:26 (NLT)

Many Christians have believed the lie that God puts sickness on people to teach them some lesson. Some have even claimed that their sickness somehow brings glory to God, yet they can offer no Scriptural evidence for their blasphemous claims. If sickness brought glory to God then why didn't He just make us **_ALL_** deformed, broken, and sickly, and then use one of His ministers to heal us miraculously and be done with it?

The simple truth is – He hasn't! Because sickness is part of the Curse and He doesn't have any of the Curse to put on us. In fact, the Curse was NEVER God's original intent for this world—love has always been God's original intent and motive because that is who He is. And just in case you haven't figured it out yet, LOVE never abuses those He loves.

1 John 4:16 declares, "And we have known and believed the love that God has for us. God is love, and he who abides in love abides in God, and God in him."

In 1 Corinthians 13 we read about LOVE'S characteristics:

> [4] Love endures long and is patient and kind; love never is envious nor boils over with jealousy, is not boastful or vainglorious, does not display itself haughtily. [5] It is not conceited (arrogant and inflated with pride); it is not rude (unmannerly) and does not act unbecomingly. Love (God's love in us) does not insist on its own rights or its own way, for

it is not self-seeking; it is not touchy or fretful or resentful; it takes no account of the evil done to it [it pays no attention to a suffered wrong]. [6] It does not rejoice at injustice and unrighteousness, but rejoices when right and truth prevail. [7] Love bears up under anything and everything that comes, is ever ready to believe the best of every person, its hopes are fadeless under all circumstances, and it endures everything [without weakening]. [8] Love never fails [never fades out or becomes obsolete or comes to an end]. (1 Corinthians 13:4-8, AMP).

The simple fact of knowing that GOD/LOVE never rejoices in injustice (verse 6), is enough to know that sickness isn't a product of God's design or will.

Where is the justice in a miscarriage, in cystic fibrosis, in cancer, or in blindness? Where's the justice in cerebral palsy, back pain, or even the common cold? There isn't any, and that's because they're not from Him.

The Bible clearly states that GOD who is LOVE never fails—He comes through and makes a way even in "impossible situations." His will is ALWAYS to see you BLESSED and WHOLE in every area of your life. When we trust God for His best He promises:

[8] …Your light shall break forth like the morning, your healing shall spring forth speedily, and your righteousness shall go before you; the glory of the LORD shall be your rear guard. [9] Then you shall call, and the LORD will answer; you shall cry, and He will say, "Here I AM." (Isaiah 58:8-9).

AMEN! Isn't it comforting to know that God is still in the business of healing, making whole, and blessing His people? God is love, and love NEVER fails. Take comfort in that fact today and believe that HE IS THE LORD THAT HEALS YOU!

Daily Declaration

Father, You are Healer, Creator, Redeemer, Protector, My Good Shepherd, and the Lover of my soul. I thank you for healing me. I praise You Father for You are so good. You love me beyond my comprehension. I don't understand it, but I receive it today.

Your great grace is in operation in my life. Help me to extend Your love to all who need to experience Your loving kindness today. Father, draw me close to Your bosom and help me to feel and to understand Your love in a tangible way. And help me to draw others to You as well.

Healing is Your specialty Abba, it doesn't really matter what is needed, You always have the perfect solution. Whether it's physical, emotional, mental, financial, relational, or all of the above—You can do what no one else can do. Moreover, You love doing it! Thank You, Thank You Thank You for Your healing anointing working deep within me and all around me.

Just as Psalm 5:12 declares, "For You, O LORD, will bless [me] the righteous; with favor, You will surround [me] as with a shield."

For I shall be like a tree planted by the rivers of water, which brings forth fruit in every season, and [my] leaves shall not wither; for whatever [I] do shall prosper in Jesus' mighty name! (See Psalm 1:3). Amen!

Day 21
He Can Heal Your Broken Heart

"He heals the broken-hearted and bandages their wounds."

Psalm 147:3 (NLT)

Emotional wounds can be nasty and remain a lifetime, if ignored or left to themselves, but the good news is that they don't have to. God is the mender of the broken-hearted, He is the restorer of the beaten and battered, and He is help to the hopeless. With God **_ALL THINGS_** truly are possible. He can take what seems like ashes and turn them into something beautiful, if you allow Him to.

Many times, when we think of healing, we forget about emotional healing and give most of our attention to the spiritual or physical healing of a person, and not the mental or emotional healing that we all need as well. But God is concerned with every detail of who you are. He cares about your spiritual, physical, mental, emotional, relational and even financial well-being. After all, He created you as a multi-faceted being just as He is a multi-faceted God.

We must remember that just as God is a triune God: Father, Son, and Holy Spirit, You and I were created in His image and are a triune being, made up of a spirit, a soul, and a body. Your spirit is the real you that lives on forever even after your physical death on earth. Your soul is the part of you that is made up of your mind, will, and emotions and enables you to think, choose, and feel. Your body, is your earthly body suit, without a physical body you do not have authority in this earthly realm.

That said, I want to focus on the part of you and me that we call the soul: your thinker, chooser, and feeler. I love the fact that Almighty God has instructed us saying:

¹⁹ I call heaven and earth as witnesses today against you, that I
have set before you life and death, blessing and cursing;
therefore **_choose life_**, that both you and your descendants may
live; ²⁰ that you may love the LORD your God, that you may
obey His voice, and that you may cling to Him, for He is your
life and the length of your days; and that you may dwell in the
land which the LORD swore to your fathers, to Abraham, Isaac,
and Jacob, to give them. (Deuteronomy 30:19-20, Emphasis
Added).

That says that we have a choice. We can either choose to allow our
circumstances to determine the way we feel, or we can choose to say,
"NO! That's not who I am." "That's not how I will remain, in Jesus'
name!" We have been given the authority to declare, "God has made me
an overcomer in Christ, and even though what I am going through right
now is not fair, and it doesn't feel good, Jesus bore this on the Cross and
I have been delivered from the Curse!"

I encourage you to Choose Life instead of death every time you face
an obstacle that doesn't line up with who Scripture says you are. You
have the choice to either lay down and accept your circumstances or to
rise up in faith, search the Bible for the precious promises concerning
your inheritance in Jesus, and start confessing them and changing your
attitude and environment.

Sure, you may have been devastated by a cheating spouse. Yes, there
is bitterness, resentment, and hurt because of that unfaithful act
committed against you. But you must decide if you want to stay bitter or
if you want to be better! Your attitude will determine which one you will
experience.

It's not fair when someone has lied about you, it hurts when
someone has been unfaithful, it can be stressful when your boss has
overlooked you for promotion for the third time, but you must train
yourself to see this bad turn of events as an opportunity for
promotion…an opportunity for personal growth.

When you experience these kinds of trials the first thing you must
determine is to believe that it's not God doing this to you in order to
teach you a lesson or punish you for your past sins. God doesn't do that

– He loves you passionately and wants you to succeed in every area of your life.

The Bible tells us it's the thief (Satan) who comes to steal, kill and destroy, but that Jesus came to give us the abundant life. (See John 10:10). The abundant life is the Blessing – the empowerment to prosper in your spirit soul, and body.

Look at 3 John 2 with me and see God's will for each and every one of His covenant children. "Beloved, I pray that you may prosper in all things and be in health, just as your soul prospers."

God wants us to be prosperous in **ALL THINGS** and to live in perfect health even as—or in proportion to, our growing in our spiritual understanding of His will (The Bible), which has the power to transform our thinking, choosing, and feeling (our soul). Look with me at Paul's prayer for us in Ephesians 1.

> [15] Therefore I also, after I heard of your faith in the Lord Jesus and your love for all the saints, [16] do not cease to give thanks for you, making mention of you in my prayers: [17] that the God of our Lord Jesus Christ, the Father of glory, may give to you the spirit of wisdom and revelation in the knowledge of Him, [18] the eyes of your understanding being enlightened; that you may know what is the hope of His calling, what are the riches of the glory of His inheritance in the saints, [19] and what is the exceeding greatness of His power toward us who believe, according to the working of His mighty power [20] which He worked in Christ when He raised Him from the dead and seated Him at His right hand in the heavenly places, [21] far above all principality and power and might and dominion, and every name that is named, not only in this age but also in that which is to come. [22] And He put all things under His feet, and gave Him to be head over all things to the church, [23] which is His body, the fullness of Him who fills all in all.

Paul's, and more importantly The Father's desire for each of us is to have the wisdom and understanding of who we are in Christ. The unsaved world may be limited by its circumstances, by the present economy, or by the negative report from the doctor, but not us. We live under a different set of rules—we are no longer slaves to the Curse, we have a glorious inheritance in Christ and a "better covenant," which has freed us from Satan's dominion and translated us into the power of God's dear son, Jesus—Hallelujah!

> [13] He has delivered us from the power of darkness and conveyed us into the kingdom of the Son of His love, [14] in whom we have redemption through His blood, the forgiveness of sins. (Colossians 1:13-14).

What would have happened to Joseph and the entire Hebrew nation if Joseph would have allowed the negative circumstances he faced to determine his future? He was betrayed by his own brothers, sold into slavery, lied and accused of rape by Potiphar's wife, thrown into prison for about thirteen years for a crime he didn't commit, forgotten about by those he helped free, until Pharaoh had a dream that no one else could interpret.

If anyone could have had a bad attitude about their circumstances, Joseph could have. But instead of looking at the negative he chose to look to God—The Author and Finisher of his faith. (See Hebrews 12:2). Instead of getting depressed and throwing in the towel by complaining and feeling sorry, Joseph chose to believe God and to fight the good fight of faith! Because of this, God took him from the pit to the palace.

You may feel like you're in the deepest pit of your life right now, but don't get bitter, get better! Don't view the negative circumstances as God trying to punish you for your past sins, but view it as an opportunity for you to triumph over the devil—over the thief, and for God to get the glory. And just like Joseph, keep trusting God, keep fighting the good fight of faith, knowing that God ALWAYS causes us to triumph in Jesus! (See 1 Corinthians 15:57 and 2 Corinthians 2:14).

You have been made the righteousness of God and you are more than a conqueror in Christ Jesus. Nothing can keep you down when You understand who you are in Christ and when you know that God will never leave you or forsake you—because you are His precious covenant Son or Daughter. Amen

Daily Declaration

Father, I thank You for Your goodness in my life! I know that in this life I will face trials, but I also know that Jesus has defeated every single one of them and made me victorious IN HIM!

You Word tells me that I am more than a conqueror in Christ (See Romans 8:37). A conqueror is someone who wins battles, but more than a conqueror means that I will never lose because I have put my faith in You, and I operate under a different set of rules than the world.

I am surrounded by Your favor as a shield (Psalm 5:12). A thousand may fall to one side and ten thousand to the other, but no harm will come near me, because I abide in You Father. (Psalm 91:7). This Scripture doesn't mean that I won't see trouble, but that trouble can't stick to me forever.

"⁴Yea, though I walk through the valley of the shadow of death, I will fear no evil; for You are with me; Your rod and Your staff, they comfort me. ⁵You prepare a table before me in the presence of my enemies; You anoint my head with oil; my cup runs over. ⁶Surely goodness and mercy shall follow me ALL the days of my life; and I will dwell in the house of the LORD forever." (Psalm 23:4-6).

In other words, I've got the victory over every negative situation and circumstance in Jesus. I refuse to cave in and quit. I refuse to allow Satan to have the last word in my life—he no longer has dominion over me—I am a new creation in Christ Jesus! And You **ALWAYS** cause me to Triumph in Jesus, AMEN!

Day 22
God Sent His WORD & Healed You & Delivered You From Your Destruction

"He sent His word and healed them, and delivered them from their destructions."

Psalm 107:20

Jesus is the Word of God personified! He is the Word that became flesh and lived among us, according to John 1:1-14. In Malachi 4:2 Jesus is called the Sun of Righteousness who comes with healing in His wings. His "wings" is a metaphor referring both to Psalm 91, which is known by many as the Psalm of protection and it also refers to the story in Mark Chapter 5, where the woman with the issue of blood touches Jesus' tallit or prayer shawl and is instantly healed.

I am so glad that this story is in the Bible. It warms my heart to see Jesus' character. After the woman touched Jesus, He asks, "Who's touched Me..." When He learns that it was the woman, and she tells Him of her condition, Jesus then says, "Daughter, your faith has made you whole (perfectly sound), go in peace (*shalom*), and be healed from your affliction."

Jesus ministry was and still is a ministry of redemption, restoration, and healing. In fact, Acts 10:38 tells us that, "God anointed Jesus of Nazareth with the Holy Spirit and with power, who went about doing good and ***HEALING ALL*** who were oppressed by the devil, for God was with Him." (Emphasis Added).

Did you see what that says? Jesus healed **_ALL_** who were oppressed by the devil. That isn't a typo or written as a sweet sentimental phrase to make us to feel warm and fuzzy inside. NO! ALL MEANS ALL!

God doesn't mince His words. He says what He means and means what He says—Period!

If you are being oppressed in any way, God's Word—Jesus, is here to deliver you from that oppression right now—even while you are reading this book. His power and authority are available for YOU this instant, to deliver you from addiction, sickness, depression, loneliness, a broken heart, whatever it is that's trying to keep you from your rightful place of victory and triumph over Satan.

In fact, if you are struggling in any area of life, I encourage you to pause for a moment and cry out to Jesus saying, "Jesus, I need you right now. I need You, to come in and rearrange my life. Deliver me Lord, from everything that is trying to hold me back from Your best. Jesus, I give my life to You and ask You to make me whole—spirit, soul, and body.

Jesus, direct my life, my relationships, my desires, my health, and lead me into the victory that You have promised in Your Word—the Bible. I need You Jesus. I love You Lord, and I ask you to intervene on my behalf, as my Lord and Savior! I pray this in Jesus' mighty name. Amen and Amen!

If you have just prayed that prayer, or one similar to it, I want you to know that the Almighty God of Heaven and The Lord, Jesus, have heard your prayer and are at work turning your situation around. God is faithful! He will never forsake you, because He loves you passionately.

This reminds me of another story captured in the pages of the Bible. The story of the crippled man lowered through the roof by his friends. In Mark 2:1-12 we read,

> And again, He [Jesus] entered Capernaum after some days, and it was heard that He was in the house. [2] Immediately many gathered together, so that there was no longer room to receive them, not even near the door. And He preached the word to them. [3] Then they came to Him, bringing a paralytic who was carried by four men. [4] And when they could not come near

Him because of the crowd, they uncovered the roof where He was. So, when they had broken through, they let down the bed on which the paralytic was lying. [5] When Jesus saw their faith, He said to the paralytic, "Son, your sins are forgiven you." [6] And some of the scribes were sitting there and reasoning in their hearts, [7] "Why does this Man speak blasphemies like this? Who can forgive sins but God alone?" [8] But immediately, when Jesus perceived in His spirit that they reasoned thus within themselves, He said to them, "Why do you reason about these things in your hearts? [9] Which is easier, to say to the paralytic, 'Your sins are forgiven you,' or to say, 'Arise, take up your bed and walk'? [10] But that you may know that the Son of Man has power on earth to forgive sins"—He said to the paralytic, [11] "I say to you, arise, take up your bed, and go to your house." [12] Immediately he arose, took up the bed, and went out in the presence of them all, so that all were amazed and glorified God, saying, "We never saw anything like this!

There is something interesting that takes place in the passage that many people overlook. There is no debate that Jesus has the power to heal, but the interesting part is how He does it. Jesus doesn't lay hands on this man, He doesn't spit in the dirt and make clay and then put it on him, No, He goes to the root cause of all sickness and disease – SIN. Before the man stands up and walks for the very first time, Jesus assures him that he is forgiven.

Why is that important? It's important because we must be able to see Jesus as the Author and Finisher of our faith (Hebrews 12:2). Our healing, salvation, and blessing doesn't come to us because of anything we have done, it's a result of what He did on the Cross. Yes, Jesus hadn't gone to the Cross yet, However, God saw His work finished from the foundation of the earth. Look at just a few of the Scriptures that point to this truth:

All who dwell on the earth will worship him, whose names have not been written in the Book of Life of the Lamb slain from the foundation of the world. (Revelation 13:8).

He indeed was foreordained before the foundation of the world, but was manifest in these last times for you. (1 Peter 1:20).

[25] And he did not enter heaven to offer himself again and again, like the high priest here on earth who enters the Most Holy Place year after year with the blood of an animal. [26] If that had been necessary, Christ would have had to die again and again, ever since the world began. But now, once for all time, he has appeared at the end of the age to remove sin by his own death as a sacrifice. (Hebrews 9:25-26, NLT).

[3-6] How blessed is God! And what a blessing he is! He's the Father of our Master, Jesus Christ, and takes us to the high places of blessing in him. Long before he laid down earth's foundations, he had us in mind, had settled on us as the focus of his love, to be made whole and holy by his love. Long, long ago he decided to adopt us into his family through Jesus Christ. (What pleasure he took in planning this!) He wanted us to enter into the celebration of his lavish gift-giving by the hand of his beloved Son. (Ephesians 1:3-6, MSG).

You see, God had a plan right from the beginning. He had a plan to save us from ourselves. You might be asking the question, *Well, if He already knew we were going to blow it, then why didn't He just make us without a free will?*

He gave us a free will because Love (who is God), always allows those He loves to choose for themselves, even to the point of rejecting the One who gave them that choice.

But getting back to my original point – Jesus forgave the paralyzed man before he received his healing. That is very important because many of us carry around the baggage of our sins – the condemnation and guilt caused through disobedience.

And Satan, the Accuser of the brethren (Revelation 12:10, Zechariah 3:1-2, Job 2:1-6), is an expert at pointing out and reminding us of our failure to obey God's commands perfectly.

As a result, when the opportunity for healing, blessing, promotion comes our way, we self-sabotage ourselves by believing the lie that we are "UNWORTHY" to receive God's Grace and unmerited favor, instead of believing in the finished work of the Cross.

Our focus is misplaced and upon ourselves, our past sins, our incapability of keeping God's LAW perfectly, instead of understanding the purpose God sent His Son in the first place. You see, God knew we couldn't keep His LAW. He knew it was impossible for fallen humanity, but He gave it to us anyway to show us what He expected and to point us to Jesus as our ONLY WAY to salvation and righteousness.

Therefore, the law was our tutor to bring us to Christ, that we might be justified by faith. (Galatians 3:24).

You see, Jesus wanted that paralytic to know that he was forgiven of ALL his sins – past, present, and future, so that the enemy could never steal his healing away from Him again.

Jesus knew that If this man's focus was on the right thing (upon Jesus and His goodness), he would never be conned into believing Satan's lies again. When Satan, came pointing his dirty fingers accusing him of his sins, the man could say, "You must not know my Jesus devil, He loves me, He's forgiven me, and He wants me blessed, healthy, and living the abundant life, in Him. So, go tell your lies to someone else – it's way too late to convince me and push me back into guilt and condemnation."

Once this man realized that He was forgiven, sin and its effects couldn't remain! They had to loose this man and flee in terror. That's why it was so easy for the man to stand when Jesus said, "Rise, pick up your bed, and walk." Satan's schemes have no weight in our lives when we know THE TRUTH! We have been forgiven. Praise God!

The same is true for you and me. We have been forgiven if we are IN CHRIST. Satan's devices are powerless against the precious blood of Jesus. The ransom for our freedom has been paid and we are now free to leave the prison that the devil has kept us in for so long.

The question is – DO YOU BELIEVE & RECEIVE THE GIFT OF GRACE AND FREEDOM OR ARE YOU GOING TO CONTINUE TO ALLOW SATAN TO CON YOU OUT OF YOUR RIGHTFUL BLESSING?

Daily Declaration

Father, Thank You for sending Your Word – Jesus, to free me from ALL of Satan's devices. Your Word Father, is life to my spirit, soul, and body, and medicine to all my flesh (Proverbs 4:20). Your Word, is a lamp to my feet and a light to my path (Psalm 119:105).

Jesus, thank you for leading me in the direction of Your goodness. I am Your sheep and You are my shepherd. I hear Your voice, obey quickly, and live in Your constant blessing. Heavenly Father, I put my faith solely in Your Word, because even when everything else in this life fails, decays, and dies, Your Word remains, thrives and produces exactly what You intended (Isaiah 40:8, Isaiah 55:11).

Father, You are my refuge and strength, I put my trust in You Only. Jesus, The Word who became flesh, The Word that You sent to heal me and deliver me from my destruction, is working mightily in me now! He is changing, rearranging, and perfecting every circumstance that concerns me. Cells, tissues, fibers, organs, bones, relationships, work related issues, and my finances are all being healed as I speak, in the mighty name of Jesus! No weapon that is formed against me will prosper (Isaiah 54:17). I break every curse and the power of every demonic force that is trying to come against me in Jesus' name!

I am Blessed in all that I do! Blessed coming in and going out. Blessed in my body, my family, my finances, and my relationships. I rest in the promises of Your Word, knowing that even in the midst of chaos, You are with me, holding me, comforting me, and letting me know that everything will be just fine. Thank You Jesus! Thank You for seeing me through and bringing me out into a glorious victory. I pray all these things in Jesus' name, Amen.

Day 23
The Lord Your Healer

"...I am the LORD who heals you."

Exodus 15:26

I'll admit, that there are times when it can be challenging to believe in a God we cannot see with our eyes and a God we cannot touch with our hands. Satan is always ready to whisper seeds of unbelief into our ears, persuading us to doubt God's existence, His love for us, and especially our worthiness to receive His grace (His unmerited and unearned favor), in our lives. He does this because he knows just how powerful faith is – it is dynamic and explosive in power.

In Matthew 17, Jesus is teaching His disciples about faith and the power of words. Jesus wants them to understand that even the tiniest amount of faith produces giant results. He isn't saying, "Now, if you want me to do this for you, you've got to muster up all the faith you can; you've got to have faith in your faith." No! He is saying, "All you have to do is believe me. Put your faith in my words, my ability, in my faith, which always produces positive results."

Jesus was clear to His disciples why they weren't getting the results they desired – it was due to unbelief creeping in and stealing the promises out from underneath them.

> He said to them, because of the littleness of your faith [that is, your lack of firmly relying trust]. For truly I say to you, if you have faith [that is living] like a grain of mustard seed, you can say to this mountain, move from here to yonder place, and it will

move; and nothing will be impossible to you. (Matthew 17:20, AMP).

I love how the Message Bible words this verse:

Because you're not yet taking God seriously," said Jesus. "The simple truth is that if you had a mere kernel of faith, a poppy seed, say, you would tell this mountain, 'Move!' and it would move. There is nothing you wouldn't be able to tackle. (Matthew 17:20, MSG)

How many of us read the Bible every single day, yet the truth of God's precious promises goes in one ear and out the other? We read verses like Exodus 15:26 which says, "…I am the LORD who heals you," and we make excuses why it's not true for us.

In the Message Bible we are told that the reason we aren't experiencing the manifestation of God's promises in our lives; is because we aren't taking God seriously. We aren't putting our faith in Jesus' faith and ability, and taking hold of the promises God has made to us.

What is it going to take for us to step out in faith and BELIEVE GOD? Is it going to take laying on a deathbed, filing for bankruptcy, standing in divorce court, or burying a child? I pray that it doesn't get to that point for you or anyone you know. I pray that you take hold of God's Word today and stand immoveable upon it until you receive exactly what was promised.

The Bible tells us that God is the Great I AM. He is Almighty God, and is whatever we need Him to be in our lives. In other words, He is unlimited, and we are unlimited when we put our faith in Him.

In Exodus 3:13-15 (NLT), we are told that God sent Moses to the people to tell them His name – I AM.

[13] But Moses protested, "If I go to the people of Israel and tell them, 'The God of your ancestors has sent me to you,' they will ask me, 'What is his name?' Then what should I tell them?" [14] God replied to Moses, "I AM WHO I AM. Say this to the people

of Israel: I AM has sent me to you." [15] God also said to Moses, "Say this to the people of Israel: Yahweh, the God of your ancestors—the God of Abraham, the God of Isaac, and the God of Jacob—has sent me to you. This is my eternal name, my name to remember for all generations.

Once we understand that EVERYTHING must bow to His name, we will be free to enjoy the true REST of faith. Faith isn't supposed to be a work, it's not supposed to be a struggle, it's not supposed to be a battle that you and I take on to conquer the devil! The battle has already been won! Satan has already been defeated, and we are the lucky ones who get to enjoy the spoils of the battle – the fruit of Jesus' work on the Cross.

Rest is the act of abstaining from labor knowing that God has already gone before us and achieved all that we have asked of Him. I love what one preacher says about rest: "When you rest, God goes to work, but when you work, God rests."

What this man of God is saying is that when you and I are laboring and trying to earn and achieve our desired results without trusting God for them, God sits down and in essence, says, "Ok, go ahead and be your own god: see how that works for you."

The Bible says, "Casting the whole of your care [all your anxieties, all your worries, all your concerns, once and for all] on Him, for He cares for you affectionately and cares about you watchfully." (1 Peter 5:7, AMP).

God is strong enough to take care of the job Himself – after all, He is the Great I AM! He doesn't need any help from us other than our faith. Faith is the only work the believer is supposed to do when it comes to spiritual matters. The promises of God are not measured by what **WE DO**, they are measured by what **JESUS HAS ALREADY DONE!** AMEN.

Jesus said, "Come to Me, all you who labor and are heavy laden, and I will give you rest." (Matthew 11:28).

Another translation says it this way:

Are you tired? Worn out? Burned out on religion? Come to me. Get away with me and you'll recover your life. I'll show you how to take a real rest. Walk with me and work with me—watch how I do it. Learn the unforced rhythms of grace. (Matthew 11:28-29, MSG).

It's high time we learn how to thrive in the unforced rhythms of grace. It's time to take God's Word seriously and take possession of all that rightfully belongs to us, in Christ.

Grace is receiving from God, all that we do not rightfully deserve because of our sin, whereas mercy is not getting what we rightfully deserve on the basis that Jesus was our legal substitute.

In other words, Jesus died in our place when He took our sins upon Himself on the Cross. He died, so that we could live free from the effects of sin, and once again walk in the blessing and full benefits of being sons and daughters of God.

Our job is to take hold of God's Word and refuse to accept anything less than what He has promised to the heirs of faith. If God has said that He is our healer, our provider, our protector, we need to believe what He's said, and take it to heart.

We must become dogmatic in our faith, trusting that He is faithful to accomplish **ALL** that He has promised! (Romans 4:21, Philippians 1:6, 1 Thessalonians 5:24). And we have got to learn to rest, knowing that if God is the Great I AM, He will certainly come through for us.

If the God of the universe can't get the job done – you and I surely can't. Why waste our time fighting a defeated foe? Jesus has already conquered sin, sickness, and every other side effect of the Curse. The battle is DONE, so, it's time to rest in Jesus and let Him work it all out for us because He loves us. Praise the Lord!

Daily Declaration

Father, thank You for saving me, for healing me, for delivering me, for prospering me, for restoring me, and for anointing me to be a light and voice to this world – illuminating Your glory to others. Help me Lord, to become steadfast in my faith and in my understanding of Your precious Word. Your Word surpasses every other voice that's ever spoken. I cling to Your promises and I establish them as the foundation for myself and for my family. Your Word has FINAL AUTHORITY in my life FOREVER!

I close my ears to the lies of the enemy, to the faulty wisdom of this fallen world, and to the chaotic noise that is constantly trying to drown out Your voice and THE TRUTH that Your Word speaks to me, as I seek You and study the Scriptures.

I rest confidently in the finished work of Jesus, knowing that I can neither add to, or take away from on the work of the Cross. Jesus said, "IT IS FINISHED!" That means my healing is complete – IN HIM. It means my peace is complete – IN HIM. It means that my prosperity is complete – IN HIM. It means that my salvation, protection, and worth are all complete – IN HIM!

I no longer need to feel like I must continually do something in order to win Your love or earn Your approval. I am already approved and loved because I am IN JESUS. Moreover, everything I need, want, and desire are already available to me – IN HIM! My only job is to believe and to receive everything Jesus has made available to me through faith, knowing that You love me and want me to have Your best! Thank You Father, I love You so much. Jesus is Lord. Amen.

Day 24
Jehovah Rapha Will Rescue You & Nurse You Back To Health

"¹God blesses those who are kind to the poor. He helps them out of their troubles. ²He protects them and keeps them alive; he publicly honors them and destroys the power of their enemies. ³He nurses them when they are sick and soothes their pains and worries."

Psalm 41:1-3 (TLB)

G od's is known as the Great Physician and as *Jehovah Rapha* which is translated as The Lord your Healer. Healing people is not something He does by chance – only if you and I are in the right place at the right time, doing the right things, with the right people. NO! Healer is just part of His character. Healing naturally flows out from Him to **ALL** who will receive it, by faith.

We looked at it earlier, however, it bears repeating. The Bible says, "And you know that God anointed Jesus of Nazareth with the Holy Spirit and with power. Then Jesus went around doing good and ***healing all*** who were oppressed by the devil, for God was with him." (Acts 10:38, NLT, Emphasis Added).

When the woman with the issue of blood encountered Jesus as He was going with Jairus, the synagogue leader, to heal his daughter who was dying from a disease, The Bible tells us:

25-29 A woman who had suffered a condition of hemorrhaging for twelve years—a long succession of physicians had treated her, and treated her badly, taking all her money and leaving her worse off than before—had heard about Jesus. She slipped in from behind and touched his robe. She was thinking to herself, "If I can put a finger on his robe, I can get well." The moment she did it, the flow of blood dried up. She could feel the change and knew her plague was over and done with. [30] At the same moment, Jesus felt energy discharging from him. He turned around to the crowd and asked, "Who touched my robe?" [31] His disciples said, "What are you talking about? With this crowd pushing and jostling you, you're asking, 'Who touched me?' Dozens have touched you!" [32-33] But he went on asking, looking around to see who had done it. The woman, knowing what had happened, knowing she was the one, stepped up in fear and trembling, knelt before him, and gave him the whole story. [34] Jesus said to her, "Daughter, you took a risk of faith, and now you're healed and whole. Live well, live blessed! Be healed of your plague. (Mark 5:25-34, MSG).

God's plan for mankind has always been for them to LIVE WELL, LIVE BLESSED, AND TO BE HEALED OF EVERY PLAGUE! This fact is documented throughout Scripture. One of my favorites, is found in John 10:10, which tells us that Satan is – the thief, and that Jesus – is the One who came to destroy the works of the devil.

The thief comes only in order to steal and kill and destroy. I came that they may have and enjoy life, and have it in abundance (to the full, till it overflows). (John 10:10, AMP).

How can a person enjoy life fully when they are under the oppression and torment of sickness, poverty, depression, fear, or any of a number of maladies caused by the Curse? The answer is: They can't! It's impossible! And that is why our Heavenly Father sent Jesus – to free us from the dominion of Satan.

The Bible tells us that, "[13] He [God] has delivered us from the power of darkness and conveyed [transferred] us into the kingdom of the Son of His love, [14] in whom we have redemption through His blood, the forgiveness of sins."

That's some amazing news! We are no longer slaves to sin, sickness, and death, because Jesus has conquered them all on the Cross. Our Daddy God, sent Him just for that reason – to set us free and to make us whole again IN HIM.

The Hebrew word *Rapha*, means to become fresh, to be completely healed or cured, to be restored, and it also refers to the work of a physician.

God is understood through His works. Though we can never fully understand who God is and define Him with human words, His miraculous works of healing and His promise to heal **ALL** who will believe on Jesus as their Savior, prove His will for all mankind concerning healing and our perfect soundness.

In Genesis 15:26 God says, "...I AM the Lord Who Heals you.

Through Isaiah 53:4-5 we understand part of Jesus' healing ministry and mission to save us from sin. The Bible says, "[4] Surely He has borne our griefs and carried our sorrows; yet we esteemed Him stricken, smitten by God, and afflicted. [5] But He was wounded for our transgressions, He was bruised for our iniquities; the chastisement for our peace was upon Him, and by His stripes we are healed."

John 3:16 explains the "WHY," of God's Amazing Grace saying, "For God so loved the world that He gave His only begotten Son, that whoever believes in Him should not perish but have everlasting life."

In John 9:1-7, we are told that sickness isn't always the result of our direct sins, but that it is the result of sin in general. In other words, sickness and disease often happen, not because God is punishing sin, but because we live in a sin infected world, which like a parasite, has worked for centuries to destroy the perfect will of God. But the good news is: if you and I are in Jesus, He has redeemed us from the Curse (Galatians 3:13-14). And if we will hold fast to His promises, He will deliver us from every symptom of the Curse, as our covenant keeping God. Hallelujah!

[1]Now as Jesus passed by, He saw a man who was blind from birth. [2]And His disciples asked Him, saying, "Rabbi, who sinned, this man or his parents, that he was born blind?" [3]Jesus answered, "Neither this man nor his parents sinned, but that the works of God should be revealed in him. [4]I must work the works of Him who sent Me while it is day; the night is coming when no one can work. [5]As long as I am in the world, I am the light of the world." [6]When He had said these things, He spat on the ground and made clay with the saliva; and He anointed the eyes of the blind man with the clay. [7]And He said to him, "Go, wash in the pool of Siloam" (which is translated, Sent). So, he went and washed, and came back seeing. (John 9:1-7).

In Psalm 147:3 we are told that, God heals the broken-hearted and binds up their wounds.

And in Proverbs 4:20-22 (AMP) we are instructed by the Lord, "[20]My son, attend to my words; consent and submit to my sayings. [21]Let them not depart from your sight; keep them in the center of your heart. [22]For they are life to those who find them, healing and health to all their flesh."

The words health and healing in verse 22, are literally rendered as medicine, remedy, and cure in the Hebrew (*marpe*). God's Word is medicine to **ALL** our flesh: spirit, soul, and body. His Word is a vaccination against the contagion that sin has caused throughout the millennia. In other words, when you take your daily dose of God's Word, meditating on His precious promises, it drives sickness and disease out of your body and brings wholeness into every area of life.

Finally, in Psalm 41:1-3 (TLB), we are told, "[1]God blesses those who are kind to the poor. He helps them out of their troubles. [2]He protects them and keeps them alive; he publicly honors them and destroys the power of their enemies. [3]He nurses them when they are sick and soothes their pains and worries."

I absolutely love the fact that God – *Jehovah Rapha* – The Lord our Healer, is described not only as the God who helps, protects, and destroys our enemies, but also as a nurse who keeps alive, heals from sickness, and soothes our pains and fears too.

Our amazing God cares and is enveloped in every aspect of our lives. He is concerned with everything that is trying to keep us from His best. He is like a mother hen who will fight to the death to protect her baby chicks.

Jesus cried and wept over His people saying, "O Jerusalem, Jerusalem! The city that murders the prophets. The city that stones those sent to help her. How often I have wanted to gather your children together even as a hen protects her brood under her wings, but you wouldn't let me."

In the book of 1 Corinthians, Jesus refers to death as the last enemy that will be destroyed. (1 Corinthians 15:26). Death has never been God's will for mankind. Sickness is part of the Curse, part of the Fall, and it has **ALL** been defeated through the death, burial, and resurrection of Jesus.

God wants you well! He wants you healed! He wants you whole in every area of life. Isn't it time to let Him be the God He wants to be in your life, and allow Him to nurse YOU back to health? I believe it is and I'm ready for all He has for you and me. Can You say Amen to that?

Daily Declaration

Father, thank You for being *Jehovah Rapah* in my life, for being my Great Physician and nursing me back to perfect health and wholeness. Thank You for ensuring that I LIVE WELL, LIVE BLESSED, AND THAT I'M HEALED AND DELIVERED FROM EVERY PLAGUE that would try to destroy my life.

I speak to sickness, disease and every symptom of the Curse and I command it to leave in Jesus' mighty name. His blood has been shed to free me from the bondage of the Curse. I receive His finished work in my body, in my health, in my finances, in my marriage, in the lives of my children, and I call those things BLESSED, in Jesus name!

Satan, as of right now, you are officially evicted and commanded to leave in Jesus' name. You are publicly charged with trespassing on God's property and will be forced to suffer the full arm of God's law. I resist you devil! I humble myself before the amazing Grace of my Almighty God – Jehovah Rapha – and you must therefore flee! (See James 4:7).

No weapon formed against me shall prosper and every evil and lying tongue that rises against me in judgement, I condemn by the authority of Jesus finished work on the Cross and His precious blood, which was shed for me. That is my right and privilege as a Son and righteous heir of God. (See Isaiah 54:17).

Now Abba Father, I just want to bless You and thank You for perfecting every circumstance and situation that concerns me. Thank You for Your unmerited favor which goes before me, behind me, and encompasses me as a shield with protection, divine health, prosperity, and Your *shalom* peace. (See Psalm 5:12).

Abba, I rest in Your promise that with long life You will satisfy me and show me Your salvation. (Psalm 91:17). I rest and put my trust in You, Daddy God, knowing that You care for me and will never allow me to be harmed. (Psalm 55:22). I am determined to rest peacefully Father, knowing that You are at work in my life, correcting everything that needs correcting and healing everything that needs healing, because You are my Amazing God and Father. Amen – So be it – In Jesus' mighty name!

Day 25
You Will Live & Not Die & Declare The Works Of The Lord!

"I shall not die, but live, and declare the works of the LORD."

Psalm 118:17

Before we get into the Word of God today, I'd like to ask you a serious question. Are You in it to win it? Yes, I know that sounds like a cliché, but it's not! I serious want to know if you are going to give God all the faith you have (His faith), to win the battle you're facing today? The reason I ask this is because, YOU must be steadfast in your faith knowing that God will do what He promised, if YOU don't give up and throw in the towel.

Is it hard at times? Certainly, but how badly do you want to poke that rotten devil in the eye and say, "Neener, neener, my God just proved you are powerless against the precious blood of Jesus and I have the victory IN HIM!

Look with me at a question Jesus asked of a man who came to him for healing.

> [35-37] He came to the outskirts of Jericho. A blind man was sitting beside the road asking for handouts. When he heard the rustle of the crowd, he asked what was going on. They told him, "Jesus the Nazarene is going by." [38] He yelled, "Jesus! Son of David! Mercy, have mercy on me!" [39] Those ahead of Jesus told the man to shut up, but he only yelled all the louder, "Son of David! Mercy, have mercy on me!" [40] Jesus stopped and ordered him to be brought over. **When he had come near, Jesus**

asked, "What do you want from me?" [41] He said, "Master, I want to see again." [42-43] Jesus said, "Go ahead—see again! Your faith has saved and healed you!" The healing was instant: He looked up, seeing—and then followed Jesus, glorifying God. Everyone in the street joined in, shouting praise to God. (Luke 18:35-43, MSG, Emphasis Added).

Do you see how important it is to know what you want from God? And not only know what you want, but be willing to fight every opposing voice that tells you to shut up, or tries to convince you that you're insignificant and not important to God.

The devil tries to do this to all of us. He tries to get us to shut up — to quit calling out to Jesus. He uses embarrassment, guilt, shame, or a host of other tactics, to try to convince us that Jesus doesn't have time for OUR ISSUE – but it's a lie! Jesus ALWAYS stops when someone places a demand on His GRACE! Praise the Lord!

We saw the same thing happen with the woman with the issue of blood, in Mark 5. Jesus was going to heal Jairus' daughter, but that woman's faith stopped Jesus in His tracks, and pulled the divine healing she so desperately desired, from Jesus.

What I'm about to say next may surprise you, but I'm going to say it anyway. Jesus isn't uptight like most people think. He's not interested in following the norms or pleasing the "religious" people. He's only concerned with pleasing the Father. It's "religious" men and women who have put heavy burdens upon the people of God – through their man-made traditions. It's the prideful and arrogant Pharisees, who have kept many of God's people from receiving the healing and blessing that He's wanted for them all along. These Pharisees have created long lists of religious rules and traditions the people must do in order to receive from Jesus. They have even set a schedule telling God when He can do them – But Jesus is ALWAYS ready to heal, save, and deliver His beloved.

Look at the following story with me and you will understand what I am saying. As a result, I pray that you will both see and reach out by faith and take all that Jesus is offering you TODAY.

> [10] Now He was teaching in one of the synagogues on the Sabbath. [11] And behold, there was a woman who had a spirit of infirmity eighteen years, and was bent over and could in no way raise herself up. [12] But when Jesus saw her, He called her to Him and said to her, "Woman, you are loosed from your infirmity." [13] And He laid His hands on her, and
> immediately she was made straight, and glorified God. [14] But the ruler of the synagogue answered with indignation, because Jesus had healed on the Sabbath; and he said to the crowd, ***"There are six days on which men ought to work; therefore, come and be healed on them, and not on the Sabbath day."*** [15] The Lord then answered him and said, "Hypocrite! Does not each one of you on the Sabbath loose his ox or donkey from the stall, and lead it away to water it? [16] ***So ought not <u>this woman, being a daughter of Abraham,</u> whom Satan has bound—think of it—for eighteen years, be loosed from this bond on the Sabbath?"*** [17] And when He said these things, all His adversaries were put to shame; and all the multitude rejoiced for all the glorious things that were done by Him.

Do you see it? The ruler of synagogue was furious with Jesus for healing on the Sabbath (the Holy Day). He should have been rejoicing at the sight of the woman's release from her bondage, but he was more concerned with his "religious laws," than he was with the miracle Jesus had done for this covenant woman.

When most people read this, they don't understand that up until the time of Jesus' ministry, people had rarely, if ever, seen miracles like this. They just didn't happen on a regular basis like they were happening with Jesus and His disciples.

This is a perfect illustration of "religion" or "having a religious spirit" – it's the act of valuing the rules and man-made traditions concerning the "how to of worship," over and above the God they claim to be worshiping.

That is why Jesus called this religious leader a hypocrite! This man's response was jaded more by jealousy and hatred and absent of love and mercy.

In Matthew chapter 9 we get a glimpse of this same religious spirit. In the story, Jesus is reaching out to the sinners and those He came to save, but the Pharisees are criticizing Him for taking the time minister to the dregs of society.

> [9] As Jesus passed on from there, He saw a man named Matthew sitting at the tax office. And He said to him, "Follow Me." So, he arose and followed Him. [10] Now it happened, as Jesus sat at the table in the house, that behold, many tax collectors and sinners came and sat down with Him and His disciples. [11] And when the Pharisees saw it, they said to His disciples, "Why does your Teacher eat with tax collectors and sinners?" [12] When Jesus heard that, He said to them, "Those who are well have no need of a physician, but those who are sick. [13] **But go and learn what this means: 'I desire mercy and not sacrifice.'** For I did not come to call the righteous, but sinners, to repentance. (Matthew 9:9-13, Emphasis Added).

God has never wanted to punish people, He has always wanted to forgive them and show them mercy. But under Old Covenant Law, He had to punish sin the way He said He would – death for disobedience. If a person obeyed they were considered righteous, but no one was able to keep His commands perfectly until Jesus came. But now that Jesus has come and fulfilled the LAW perfectly, we have inherited the blessing and unmerited favor He deserves, and He took all the punishment you and I deserved. Therefore, Mercy and Grace have been made available to everyone who will put their trust in Him through faith.

I want you to know that His grace and mercy extends to every facet of your life. It extends to your finances, the salvation of your loved ones, your mental and emotional soundness and even to the perfect soundness and healing of your body.

His desire is to see you BLESSED and lacking NO GOOD THING! The Bible declares over and over:

> [8] Oh, put God to the test and see how kind he is! See for yourself the way his mercies shower down on all who trust in him. [9] If you belong to the Lord, reverence him; for everyone who does this has everything he needs. [10] Even strong young lions sometimes go hungry, but those of us who reverence the Lord will never lack any good thing. (Psalm 34:8-10, TLB).

> The LORD God is our protector and glorious king. He blesses us with kindness and honor. The LORD freely gives every good thing to those who do what is right [to those who have been made righteous in Jesus, 1 Cor. 15:21]. (Psalm 84:11).

> [2] But unto you who revere and worshipfully fear My name shall the Sun of Righteousness arise with healing in His wings and His beams, and you shall go forth and gambol [frolic], like calves [released] from the stall and leap for joy. [3] And you shall tread down the lawless and wicked, for they shall be ashes under the soles of your feet in the day that I shall do this, says the Lord of hosts. (Malachi 4:2-3, AMP).

You see, our job is to rest and believe God. The Lord's job is to do exactly what He promised He would do in the Bible. If He's promised something, it will come to pass – you can count on it! Why worry and stress over something that is already being perfected while you rest?

[33] But seek (aim at and strive after) first of all His kingdom and His righteousness (His way of doing and being right), and then all these things taken together will be given you besides. [34] So do not worry or be anxious about tomorrow, for tomorrow will have worries and anxieties of its own. Sufficient for each day is its own trouble. (Matthew 6:33-34, AMP).

That said, let's turn our attention back to the Scripture we looked at in the beginning of today's devotion.

"I shall not die, but live, and declare the works of the LORD." (Psalm 118:17).

Now, I asked you earlier if you were in it to win it – remember? I don't care if you have received a bad report from the doctor. I don't care if your body is screaming at you, and I don't care if the devil is telling you that he's going to take you out this time through whatever it is you are facing.

What I do care about, is who's report you're going to believe! Will you choose to believe God or all the other lying forces that are trying to kill you and take you out?

Don't get me wrong, I am sympathetic to what you are going through, but now isn't the time to lay down and die. It's the time to stand up and boldly declare, **"My God is for me, who dare come against me! (Romans 8:31). With long life my God will satisfy me and show me His salvation (Psalm 91:16). "I shall not die, but live, and declare the works of the LORD." (Psalm 118:17).**

Hallelujah! Let God be true and every man a liar! (Romans 3:4).

Daily Declaration

Father, I thank You for Your Mercy and Great Grace that goes before me. I am grateful that You desire mercy over sacrifice and that Jesus is, and was the ONE-TIME sacrifice for everything I have need of. I am SAVED, HEALED, DELIVERED, and BLESSED IN HIM ALONE! My good works and even my sins do not govern my outcome – I am eternally saved and whole in Jesus!

ABBA, I am in it to win it! I am not moved by what I hear, see, or feel. I am only moved by the precious promises found in Your Word! I take possession today, of **_ALL_** the promises You have made concerning my healing and my blessing. I establish them as the foundation for the great turn-around that is taking place, even as I pray this prayer today.

I decree that I shall live and not die, and I will declare the mighty works of My God and My Savior Jesus! I speak healing, wholeness, and restoration to every cell, tissue, fiber, organ, muscle, and bone in my body! Body, listen up and obey the Word of the Lord – YOU ARE HEALED, IN JESUS' NAME!

Blood pressure, glucose levels, airways and lungs, veins and arteries, heart, liver, thyroid, and mind, I command you to function perfectly – regulate and do what you were created to do, NOW – IN JESUS' MIGHTY NAME!

The Lord is my shepherd and I shall not want, because I already possess everything I have need or desire of, in Jesus! (Psalm 23:1). I am the righteousness of God, and I shall lack no good thing, in Jesus' name! The world may lack, the unsaved may suffer, but I have a covenant with Almighty God. He has promised to be my source and supply for all things! With long life He will satisfy me and show me His salvation (All the intricacies and beauty of my Lord, Jesus). Amen and Amen!

Day 26
A Thousand Will Fall To Your Side, But No Harm Will Come Near You

"[7] Though a thousand fall at my side, though ten thousand are dying around me, the evil will not touch me. [8] I will see how the wicked are punished, but I will not share it. [9] For Jehovah is my refuge! I choose the God above all gods to shelter me. [10] How then can evil overtake me or any plague come near? [11] For he orders his angels to protect me wherever I go."

Psalm 91:7-11 (TLB)

Today, I want to focus on the power of God's covenant promises. Though we have studied this before, it is imperative that we both believe and understand the authority of Scripture. God never says things He doesn't mean and He ALWAYS makes good on the promises He's made to His covenant children, if they dare to take Him at His word and believe.

I would venture to guess that most of the people reading this book, know Psalm 91 as the "Protection Psalm." In fact, many Christians give copies of this Psalm to loved ones going away to serve in the military. Others, inscribe it on the inside of cards or books given to those going through difficult seasons of life, as an encouragement for them to keep trusting God, to give them victory in their struggles.

These gestures are wonderful, but the problem is that most of the people who both give and receive these promises from Psalm 91, don't truly believe what is being said. They view the Bible as a kind and sentimental word of encouragement instead of as GOD'S REAL PROMISES TO THEM.

In other words, they do not believe that if something bad were to happen, that God would save them, even while unsaved people around them were maimed and even killed.

But the Bible repeatedly says that our God, is a God who brings to pass every promise He makes! God's Word confirms that His precious promises will ALWAYS come to pass just as He spoke them.

> God is not a man, that He should lie, nor a son of man, that He should repent. Has He said, and will He not do? Or has He spoken, and will He not make it good? (Numbers 23:19).

> In the same way, my words leave my mouth, and they don't come back without results. My words make the things happen that I want to happen. They succeed in doing what I send them to do. (Isaiah 55:11, ERV).

> For I am the LORD. I speak, and the word which I speak will come to pass; it will no more be postponed; for in your days, O rebellious house, I will say the word and perform it," says the Lord GOD. (Ezekiel 12:25).

> But whatever is good and perfect comes to us from God, the Creator of all light, and he shines forever without change or shadow. (James 1:17, TLB).

I believe that our Heavenly Father wants our faith to come up to a higher level. I believe He wants us to know Him by His Word – Through His precious promises, and for us to believe His promises more than we believe in things like gravity and more than we believe in our next breath.

He wants us to look to Him in every situation! Not only as God, but as Savior, Protector, Provider, Healer and Father too. God isn't some distant Creator, who has no interest in His creation. He is a loving Father, who is desperately in love with, and concerned with each and every detail of our lives. He wants to know us intimately and share life with us on a daily basis.

And when it comes to His covenant promises, He wants us to know that He ALWAYS honors His Word. There is a saying that I used to hear frequently when I was a kid. When a person was describing a person you could trust, they would say: That person's word is their bond. It is the same way with God, but God cannot lie – men do lie, and break promises.

In fact, the Bibles tells us that when God makes a promise, His oath is backed by the highest and most precious guarantee – Himself.

> [16]...By Myself I have sworn, says the LORD, because you have done this thing, and have not withheld your son, your only son— [17]blessing I will bless you… (Genesis 22:16-17).

> For when God made a promise to Abraham, because He could swear by no one greater, He swore by Himself. (Hebrews 6:13).

You might be asking yourself the question, *What's the big deal, Mike?* The big deal is that God's promises are all backed with His own life. A covenant promise, is the highest oath any individual can ever make. And Biblical covenants are ALWAYS ratified in blood, which is the symbol for both life and death. (See Leviticus 17:11 and Genesis 4:10). That is why animal sacrifice and ultimately Jesus death on the Cross, was so important for the atonement and remission of sin.

If God (The Father), were to ever break a covenant promise, then He would then be forced of His own will, to die for breaking His covenant Word – but thank you Jesus, that will never happen.

I hope that you now, understand the gravity of God's promises to us. He doesn't flippantly say things He doesn't mean. Every word He speaks has meaning and value. And that is why Psalm 91 is so important for today's study. Let's look at it again.

> [7] Though a thousand fall at my side, though ten thousand are dying around me, the evil will not touch me. [8] I will see how the wicked are punished, but I will not share it. [9] For Jehovah is my refuge! I choose the God above all gods to shelter me. [10] How then can evil overtake me or any plague come near? [11] For he orders his angels to protect me wherever I go. (Psalm 91:7-11).

When all hell is breaking loose around you, when sickness, disease, financial ruin, divorce, and tragedy are all trying to get you to doubt God's love and His presence in your life, you can look no further than this precious promise, and know that God cannot and will not fail you!

Even if a global epidemic or a nuclear catastrophe were to occur, you could stand on this promise knowing that God would protect you and all of your loved ones, even when thousands all around you were dropping like flies.

I don't mean to sound heartless or uncaring by using the phrase, "dropping like flies," I am simply trying to state a truth. God's people aren't subjected to the same circumstances that the unsaved world is. We have preferential treatment because of our relationship with Jesus! We have diplomatic immunity in a sense. God will change and even temporarily rearrange the natural laws of physics and science to ensure that His promises to you are kept. Look with me at these two examples below:

The first story we will look at is about Joshua who is helping the Gibeonites defeat the Amorites. They're winning the battle against their enemies, but the day is passing quickly. Joshua prays and asks God to keep the sun from setting to ensure that no remnant of the Amorites escape from the sword, due to the setting of the sun.

> [6] The Gibeonites then sent word to Joshua in the camp at Gilgal: "Do not abandon your servants. Come up to us quickly and save us! Help us, because all the Amorite kings from the hill country have joined forces against us." [7] So Joshua marched up from Gilgal with his entire army, including all the best fighting men. [8] The LORD said to Joshua, "Do not be afraid of them; I have given them into your hand. Not one of them will be able to

withstand you." ⁹After an all-night march from Gilgal, Joshua took them by surprise. ¹⁰The LORD threw them into confusion before Israel, so Joshua and the Israelites defeated them completely at Gibeon. Israel pursued them along the road going up to Beth Horon and cut them down all the way to Azekah and Makkedah. ¹¹As they fled before Israel on the road down from Beth Horon to Azekah, the LORD hurled large hailstones down on them, and more of them died from the hail than were killed by the swords of the Israelites. *¹²On the day the LORD gave the Amorites over to Israel, Joshua said to the LORD in the presence of Israel: "Sun, stand still over Gibeon, and you, moon, over the Valley of Aijalon." ¹³So the sun stood still, and the moon stopped, till the nation avenged itself on its enemies, as it is written in the Book of Jashar. The sun stopped in the middle of the sky and delayed going down about a full day. ¹⁴There has never been a day like it before or since, a day when the LORD listened to a human being. Surely the LORD was fighting for Israel! ¹⁵Then Joshua returned with all Israel to the camp at Gilgal.* (Joshua 10:6-15, NIV).

God extended the day for Joshua, because Joshua was His covenant man. Moreover, **ALL** of the Israelites returned to Gilgal. Not even one of them died in battle. This story is not only written in the Bible, but there is also historical proof of its reliability and validity in the book of Jashar – a non-canonical (or non-biblical) historical book.

The second story I want you to see, deals with the preferential treatment that the Hebrews experienced while they were slaves in Egypt. They were supernaturally delivered from experiencing the global plagues that **ALL** of the Egyptians experienced, because they were God's covenant people.

During the Ten Plagues Egypt faced because Pharaoh wouldn't let the Hebrews go to the Promised Land, we discover:

The only place it did not hail was the land of Goshen, where the Israelites were. (Exodus 9:26, NIV).

Then during the ninth plague – The plague of darkness, found in Exodus chapter 10, we read:

> [21] Then the LORD said to Moses, "Stretch out your hand toward heaven, that there may be darkness over the land of Egypt, darkness which may even be felt." [22] So Moses stretched out his hand toward heaven, and there was thick darkness in all the land of Egypt three days. [23] They did not see one another; nor did anyone rise from his place for three days. ***But all the children of Israel had light in their dwellings.***" (Exodus 10:21-23).

And finally, the Tenth Plague – The First Passover, which we read about in Exodus chapters 11:4-7 and 12:3-13

> [4] Then Moses said, "Thus says the LORD: 'About midnight I will go out into the midst of Egypt; [5] and all the firstborn in the land of Egypt shall die, from the firstborn of Pharaoh who sits on his throne, even to the firstborn of the female servant who is behind the handmill, and all the firstborn of the animals. [6] Then there shall be a great cry throughout all the land of Egypt, such as was not like it before, nor shall be like it again. [7] But against none of the children of Israel shall a dog move its tongue, against man or beast, ***that you may know that the LORD does make a difference between the Egyptians and Israel…***
>
> [3] [Moses] Speak to all the congregation of Israel, saying: 'On the tenth of this month every man shall take for himself a lamb, according to the house of his father, a lamb for a household. [4] And if the household is too small for the lamb, let him and his neighbor next to his house take it according to the number of the persons; according to each man's need you shall make your count for the lamb. [5] Your lamb shall be without blemish, a male of the first year. You may take it from the sheep or from the goats. [6] Now you shall keep it until the fourteenth day of the same month. Then the whole assembly of the congregation of Israel shall kill it at twilight. [7] And they shall take some of the

blood and put it on the two doorposts and on the lintel of the houses where they eat it. [8] Then they shall eat the flesh on that night; roasted in fire, with unleavened bread and with bitter herbs they shall eat it. [9] Do not eat it raw, nor boiled at all with water, but roasted in fire—its head with its legs and its entrails. [10] You shall let none of it remain until morning, and what remains of it until morning you shall burn with fire. [11] And thus you shall eat it: with a belt on your waist, your sandals on your feet, and your staff in your hand. So, you shall eat it in haste. It is the LORD's Passover. [12] 'For I will pass through the land of Egypt on that night, and will strike all the firstborn in the land of Egypt, both man and beast; and against all the gods of Egypt I will execute judgment: I am the LORD. [13] Now the blood shall be a sign for you on the houses where you are. ***And when I see the blood, I will pass over you; and the plague shall not be on you to destroy you when I strike the land of Egypt.***

I hope you are getting this! God's covenant people are not limited or bound by the same laws unsaved people are bound by.

If the doctor has given you a bad report, thank him for his expert opinion and then say, "My God is bigger than this negative report doc, God is already at work, healing my body and making the crooked places straight. Jesus died so that I could live and thrive. His blood was shed for my salvation and for my healing and therefore, God will honor Jesus' sacrifice just like He honored the blood the Hebrews put on the doorposts of their homes in Egypt. But Jesus' blood speaks louder than a natural lamb's blood. He is the Lamb who was sacrificed from the foundation of the world, just for this purpose. Hallelujah!"

Jesus told his disciples (including you and me), that we may be in the world, but we are not of it. (See John 17:16). The Message Bible says it this way:

Now I'm returning to you. I'm saying these things in the world's hearing, so my people can experience My joy completed in them. I gave them your word; the godless world hated them because of it, ***because they didn't join the world's ways, just as I didn't*** *join the world's ways.* I'm not asking that you take them out of the world but that you guard them from the Evil One. ***They are no more defined by the world than I am defined by the world.*** Make them holy—consecrated—with the truth; Your word is consecrating truth. (John 17:13-16, MSG, Emphasis Added).

Look what Satan had to say about God's covenant protection:

Satan retorted, "So do you think Job does all that out of the sheer goodness of his heart? ***Why, no one ever had it so good! You pamper him like a pet, make sure nothing bad ever happens to him or his family or his possessions, bless everything he does—he can't lose!*** (Job 1:9-10, MSG, Emphasis Added).

If we would just dare to believe the Word of God – I mean really believe it – we would begin to experience miracles like never before. God's Word is the SUPREME TRUTH of the universe and NOTHING surpasses it in might or strength.

I encourage you to believe in the supernatural truth that no weapon formed against you shall prosper because God is a covenant keeping God. (See Isaiah 54:17).

I beg you to believe that, By His stripes YOU WERE (past tense) Healed! (See 1 Peter 2:24). And if YOU WERE HEALED – THEN YOU STILL ARE! There are no expiration dates on God's Words – Hallelujah!

And finally, I dare YOU – No, I double dog dare YOU, to really believe that, although a thousand may fall at your side, and ten thousand at your right hand; **NO HARM** will come near you…because you have made the Lord JESUS, your refuge, the Most High God, your dwelling place, **NO EVIL** shall happen to you, nor will any plague come near your dwelling, IN JESUS' MIGHTY NAME! AMEN!

Daily Declaration

Heavenly Father, I thank You today for Your covenant Word. Your Word never returns to You without producing exactly what You spoke it into existence to accomplish. I am grateful that Your Word works for me when I speak it, just like it works for You.

I decree and declare that even if a thousand should fall to one side and ten thousand to the other, no harm shall come near me or my family, because I have put my trust in Jesus. His blood has sealed me and delivered me from the hands of Satan. No weapon that the enemy forms against me shall prosper, because my covenant keeping God has delivered and will continually deliver me from all destruction.

Father, I thank You that I am not limited by this world's limits. I am not defined by the world's ways, and I refuse to join in with them. Jesus has delivered me from the dominion of the devil. Just as Satan said of Job: "No one has ever had it so good! You pamper me like a pet, You make sure nothing bad ever happens to me or my family or my possessions, You bless everything I do—I just can't lose! Because Jesus is my Lord and Savior! Hallelujah!

And just like Joshua and the Hebrews in Goshen, I have diplomatic immunity from economic depression, sickness and disease, and every other crisis that this unsaved world faces, because I trust only in You Lord. You are my refuge and hope!

Father, Your Word is a lamp to my feet and a light on my path. I choose to believe every single word, even when I do not understand how it is humanly possible. Help me Lord to take hold of it and thereby, take hold of You, and experience the goodness of the Lord in the land of the living (See Psalm 27:13).

Day 27
Avoid FEAR At All Costs!

"For God has not given us a spirit of fear, but of power and of love and of a sound mind."

2 Timothy 1:7

Do You know what the greatest hindrance to faith is? It's Fear. Fear will steal your confidence, and make you doubt God's promises, to the point that they won't work in your life. Does this mean that fear is more powerful than faith? Of course not! But our Amazing God has given each of us the ability to either take hold of His promises or reject them, by giving us a free-will.

Let me ask you a question. What is the first thing everyone experiences the moment they get a bad report? FEAR! Satan tries to use fear to move us from the firm foundation of God's holy Word, to a place of doubt and unbelief. He knows that if he can convince us to believe in the "facts" or "lies" he is presenting, instead of the TRUTH of God's Word, He's won the battle.

Did you catch what I said? I said "FACTS" or "LIES" instead of "THE TRUTH." I know that may sound a little confusing, but let me explain.

As an example, let's say you lost your job today and that you were the sole bread winner. One of the first things that would come to your mind would be: *How in the world am I going to make it?* Or maybe the thought: *Oh my goodness, I'm going to lose my home and my family will have to live on the streets…what am I going to do?*

That's exactly, how the enemy wants us to respond – to think – *What am I going to do?* But that's the problem! As a covenant child of God, **YOU ARE NOT YOUR SOURCE – GOD IS!**

Yet, Satan knows, that if he can get your eyes off of God – off of the promises found in the Bible – and on to yourself, you are defeated. That is the whole tactic of fear. To drive you away from faith and get you frantically working to provide for yourself.

Bear with me as I share a real-life story about my mother that will help you understand my point. One morning I was on the road visiting some of my clients, when I received a call from my mom.

"Mike, I just got off the phone with my boss. She said the funding has been pulled from my department and they are laying the entire crew off, effective immediately! I quit my old job last week to take this one, and now it's over. What am I gonna do?!" Her voice was trembling, and she was breathing fast. I could tell she was very near tears.

But I had been feeding on teaching CD's (sermons) from several of my favorite pastors, and I was full of the Word and brimming over with faith. I knew I needed to stop the fear and get her on the Word immediately.

"Mom, hold on a minute, just think, what is different right this minute, from when you went to bed last night?"

I could hear a rush of breath when she exclaimed, "I just TOLD you what's different! Last night, I had a job. As of five minutes ago, I don't, and I have no savings, NOTHING! How am I going to make it 'til I find another job? You can't help me, you've got your own family. What can I do?"

She was very close to hysteria and I could understand why, she had my little sister to take care of and they'd been having a hard time lately. And although I understood her fear and felt for her, I couldn't give in. I had to get her back on the Word if she was going to receive her victory in this.

So, I took a deep breath and calmly stated, "You've been studying and reading your Bible haven't you?"

"Yes, of course!" she said, "but..."

"There are no "buts" with God! Either His Word is true, or it's not. Which is it? Do you believe Him when He says He's your Provider...? When He says FEAR NOT...?! When He says He provides for the birds of the air, how much more will He take care of you...? When He says, "And My God shall supply ALL your need according to His riches in Christ Jesus...?

I thought I was drawing her back in and that she was starting to come around and understand what I was saying to her...But SUDDENLY....

"Never mind, I'll talk to you later." And she hung up.

I immediately started praying for her and her situation, but thought it was best if I let her cool off and catch her breath. The problem was real, I'd been in here shoes before, and I knew she was panicking, but that's what fear does, it torments you and causes you to think the worst.

The Bible tells us, "There is no fear in love [who is God]; but perfect love casts out fear, because fear involves torment. But he who fears has not been made perfect [mature] in love [who is God]." (1 John 4:18).

Fears number one goal is to cause you to cast everything you say you believe out the window and run around like a chicken with your head cut off – trying to take care of yourself. But faith rests in God's promises trusting that He will do EXACTLY what He's promised in the Bible.

At 4:00 pm that same day, I received a call back from my mom who now seemed a little more calm.

She said, "You're never going to believe this..."

I interrupted saying, "Yes, I will mom, I'm a BELIEVER."

"Well, this morning when I called you, I was so mad at you because you were so calm when I was telling you what had just happened. It seemed as if you didn't even care about what I was telling you. You just kept talking about what the Bible said, and it was making me mad. I didn't see how what the Bible said, could help with my immediate needs. But this afternoon I received another call from the same person at my new job saying that they had just found some more money in the budget, and they want me to report to work tomorrow after all."

"Hallelujah! Isn't God good!" I said.

"I want you to know, I have spent most of the day frantically trying to figure out what I could do about finding another job. I've been mad at you, mad at God, and scared that your little sister and I would have nowhere to live. But after all my efforts failed, I stopped, took a breath, and just began to cry. As I was crying, I was telling God what you had said to me on the phone this morning: that He'd promised to be my source and supply. (Philippians 4:19). That He'd made a covenant to take care of us. (Isaiah 41:10). That the Bible promises that even when we go through trials, we are to be of good cheer, because Jesus has overcome those trials for us. (See John 16:33). And He heard me Mike…He heard, and He answered my prayers. Not only did He hear them, but He answered them all in the same day. **I WILL NEVER FORGET THIS**, for as long as I live. I now understand what you were trying to tell me. It's become **REAL** to me today. I'm sorry for hanging up on you."

"That's the problem mom, most of us wait until all else has failed, to include God in our circumstances. If He is God, He should be the first one we go to for everything."

We spent the next twenty minutes talking about the miracle God had just done for my mom. We cried with joy, and laughed at the devil, and gave the Lord praise for His goodness.

I hope you remember this the next time Satan comes at you and tries to get you to fear. You need to recognize what's happening, remember that God hasn't given you the spirit of fear, but He's given you a spirit of love, power, and a sound mind. If you trust Jesus – He will see you through to your victory! Amen.

Daily Declaration

Father, I thank You for being my Source and Supply in **_ALL_** things. You are my God and I know that You love me and will always take good care of me. Lord, help me to trust in You at all times. Even when bad reports and opportunities for me to enter into fear come my way. I am a believer, and I choose to believe You!

I rebuke fear and cast down every imagination that would try to exalt itself above the knowledge of You Jesus, and Your precious promises in the Bible. (2 Corinthians 10:5).

Your Word is **THE HIGHEST FORM OF TRUTH** (John 17:17). There is nothing greater than Your Word Father. Your Word will change situations and circumstances, if necessary, to see me through.

Help me Lord, to feed my spirit with Your precious Word each and every day. Your Word is life and health to all my flesh. It's the source that produces faith in my spirit. And it will help me to overcome every obstacle in this life.

Revelation 12:11 says, "And they overcame him by the blood of the Lamb and by the word of their testimony…" Lord, help me to make sure that the words I speak are the words that You have already spoken to me in the Bible. Help me to see myself as You see me and to say only what You have already said about me. I am the righteousness of God in Jesus (2 Corinthians 5:21).

I don't care what the world thinks of me, because I am not of this world. I am Yours and I am only concerned with pleasing You. Every time fear comes my way, help me to remember this wonderful promise from Your Word:

> Fear not, for I am with you; be not dismayed, for I am your God. I will strengthen you, yes, I will help you, I will uphold you with My righteous right hand. (Isaiah 41:10).

I pray all of this in the mighty name of Jesus' Amen!

Day 28
He Will Take Away All Sickness

"And ye shall serve the LORD your God, and he shall bless thy bread, and thy water; and I will take sickness away from the midst of thee."

Exodus 23:25 (KJV)

As we have discussed earlier, God isn't the One who puts sickness on people, but He is the One who heals and delivers them. Those who belong to Him, by accepting Jesus as Lord and Savior, are the ones who serve the Lord.

When we talk about serving the Lord, it has to do with being a member of His family – Being a covenant child – and worshiping Him and Him alone as God and Father.

The Hebrew word *abad*, which is translated as "serve" in Exodus 23:25 means, "to perform acts of worship, to be employed as a member, to obey, or to be a slave to."

Through Christ Jesus, we have all become these things. We are members of the Body of Christ. We have performed acts of worship by choosing Jesus as our personal Savior. And we continue to serve Him when we follow His commands. We have also all obeyed every one of God's Laws perfectly – In Christ. We haven't done that on our own, nor could we ever do it apart from Jesus, but we have done it – IN HIM. In other words, He did it for us and we reap the benefits of His perfect obedience.

I want you to know that God sees you and me the same way He sees Jesus. He sees us sinless and perfect! Not because you and I are good – we're not! But **Jesus IS** the perfect and sinless lamb of God, who came and died **to make us righteous** and free from the dominion of sin and the Curse. (See John 3:16, Galatians 3:13-14, and Colossians 1:13). We are perfect in Jesus, but apart from Him we are doomed to hell.

Let's look again at our verse of the day.

> And ye shall serve the LORD your God, and he shall bless thy bread, and thy water; and I will take sickness away from the midst of thee. (Exodus 23:25).

Every time I see this verse it reminds me not of what I need to do to try to earn God's blessing in my life, ***but what Jesus has already done for me and you*** in His sacrifice on the Cross.

You see, I know that I'm already In Christ, and therefore, serving Him. So, now, my attention then moves to the next part of that verse, the part that God does: "…He shall bless thy bread, and thy water; and [He will] take sickness away from the midst of thee."

He will BLESS my food and my water… What does that mean? In a very basic sense, it means that He will multiply it, heal it, transform, and even make it more nutritious.

To bless something, is to do something good or to empower it to prosper. But when I read this Scripture I think of something else too. It always reminds me of communion – The Lord's Supper.

Even though this Scripture doesn't say it directly, I always think of Exodus 23:25 as God telling me: **"And I shall BE your healing bread and water, and I will take sickness from your midst."**

After all, Jesus is the Bread of Life (See John 6:25-59). And in John 4:14, Jesus said, "But whoever drinks of the water that I shall give him will never thirst. But the water that I shall give him will become in him a fountain of water springing up into everlasting life."

Jesus' nature is to give and to bless. Everyone He ever met, left better off than they were prior to meeting Him. They all went away with full bellies (Matthew 14:13-21, Mark 8:1-10), The blind went away seeing (John 9:1-34, Mark 8:22-25, Luke 18:35-43), and the lame walking (Matthew 9:1-8, John 5:1-47). The lepers were made whole (Matthew

8:1-4, Luke 17:11-19), and the sick restored to health (Matthew 8:5-13, Mark 3:1-6, Mark 5:21-43, Luke 8:43-48).

Our healing, doesn't cost us a thing. We can't pay enough to get it and we can't do enough "righteous works" to earn it. But it did cost Jesus – It cost Him His life.

One of the ways you and I honor His sacrifice on the Cross is by taking the communion elements in remembrance of Him. This isn't just a "religious" act, but it's an act of worship. It's also a method by which many people I know have received their healing. In fact, I have received healing in my own body through communion.

In Matthew 26:26-28, we find Jesus instituting the Lord's Supper, "[26] And as they were eating, Jesus took bread, blessed and broke it, and gave it to the disciples and said, "Take, eat; this is My body." [27] Then He took the cup, and gave thanks, and gave it to them, saying, "Drink from it, all of you. [28] For this is My blood of the new covenant, which is shed for many for the remission of sins.

So that we are clear about what each of the elements represents, I want to look at a few verses of Scripture. Here in Matthew 26, Jesus says that the bread was broken and given to the disciples to eat as a symbol of His body, and the wine was a symbol of His blood, for the remission of sins.

In John chapter 6, Jesus calls Himself the Bread from Heaven who gives life to the world. So, then bread represents life and wholeness, or we could even say healing and rejuvenation to our sin infected bodies.

> [32] Then Jesus said to them, "Most assuredly, I say to you, Moses did not give you the bread from heaven, but My Father gives you the true bread from heaven. [33] For the bread of God is He who comes down from heaven and gives life to the world." [34] Then they said to Him, "Lord, give us this bread always." [35] And Jesus said to them, "I am the bread of life. He who comes to Me shall never hunger, and he who believes in Me shall never thirst. [36] But I said to you that you have seen Me and yet do not believe. (John 6:32-36).

There is an Old Testament story that may help us understand this better. During the Exodus from Egypt, Moses was leading the people through the desert towards the promised land. As they are traveling through the arid terrain, they were in need of food and water. The people were complaining and asking Moses if he had brought them into the desert to kill them. And when they finally found water, it was too bitter to drink – it was putrid water.

> [22] So Moses brought Israel from the Red Sea; then they went out into the Wilderness of Shur. And they went three days in the wilderness and found no water. [23] Now when they came to *Marah*, they could not drink the waters of *Marah*, for they were bitter. Therefore, the name of it was called *Marah* [bitter]. [24] And the people complained against Moses, saying, "What shall we drink?" [25] **So he cried out to the LORD, and <u>the LORD showed him a tree. When he cast it into the waters, the waters were made sweet.</u>** (Exodus 15:22-25, Emphasis Added).

The tree that Moses cast into the bitter waters of *Marah* was a symbol of the Cross that Jesus would be crucified upon. When Jesus is added to anything dead or cursed – healing takes place.

If we continue in Exodus chapter 16, we find another interesting symbol – Bread from Heaven.

> [1] And they journeyed from Elim, and all the congregation of the children of Israel came to the Wilderness of Sin, which is between Elim and Sinai, on the fifteenth day of the second month after they departed from the land of Egypt. [2] Then the whole congregation of the children of Israel complained against Moses and Aaron in the wilderness. [3] And the children of Israel said to them, "Oh, that we had died by the hand of the LORD in the land of Egypt, when we sat by the pots of meat *and* when we ate bread to the full! For you have brought us out into this wilderness to kill this whole assembly with hunger." [4] Then the

LORD said to Moses, "Behold, *I will rain bread from heaven for you*. And the people shall go out and gather a certain quota every day, that I may test them, whether they will walk in My law or not. [5] And it shall be on the sixth day that they shall prepare what they bring in, and it shall be twice as much as they gather daily." [6] Then Moses and Aaron said to all the children of Israel, "At evening you shall know that the LORD has brought you out of the land of Egypt. [7] And in the morning, you shall see the glory of the LORD; for He hears your complaints against the LORD. But what are we, that you complain against us?" [8] Also Moses said, *"This shall be seen when the LORD gives you meat to eat in the evening, and in the morning bread to the full; for the LORD hears your complaints* which you make against Him. And what *are* we? Your complaints *are* not against us but against the LORD." [9] Then Moses spoke to Aaron, "Say to all the congregation of the children of Israel, 'Come near before the LORD, for He has heard your complaints.'" [10] Now it came to pass, as Aaron spoke to the whole congregation of the children of Israel, that they looked toward the wilderness, and behold, the glory of the LORD appeared in the cloud. [11] And the LORD spoke to Moses, saying, [12] "I have heard the complaints of the children of Israel. Speak to them, saying, *'At twilight you shall eat meat, and in the morning, you shall be filled with bread.* And you shall know that I *am* the LORD your God.'" [13] So it was that quails came up at evening and covered the camp, and in the morning the dew lay all around the camp. [14] And when the layer of dew lifted, there, on the surface of the wilderness, was a small round substance, *as* fine as frost on the ground. [15] So when the children of Israel saw *it*, they said to one another, "What is it?" For they did not know what it *was*. And Moses said to them, *"This is the bread which the LORD has given you to eat."* (Exodus 15:22-16:23, Emphasis Added).

When God's people were thirsty, He provided water, when they were hungry, He provided bread and meat. God is *Jehovah Jireh* – The Lord our provider. Why is it so hard for us to believe that when we are sick, He will provide healing for our body, soul, and spirit?

Jesus is the Bread of Life – bread was and still is a basic part of life in the near east. Jesus, by calling Himself the Bread of life, was calling Himself the essential foundation for life. In other words, life springs from Him. If we want life, we must partake of Him.

Jesus affirmed this truth in John 6:53, when He said, "Most assuredly, I say to you, unless you eat the flesh of the Son of Man and drink His blood, you have no life in you."

Finally, in 1 Corinthians 11:23-30 Paul gives the church instructions regarding the receiving of the communion elements.

> [23] For I received from the Lord that which I also delivered to you: that the Lord Jesus on the same night in which He was betrayed took bread; [24] and when He had given thanks, He broke it and said, "Take, eat; this is My body which is broken for you; do this in remembrance of Me." [25] In the same manner He also took the cup after supper, saying, "This cup is the new covenant in My blood. This do, as often as you drink it, in remembrance of Me." *[26] For as often as you eat this bread and drink this cup, you proclaim the Lord's death till He comes. [27] Therefore whoever eats this bread or drinks this cup of the Lord in an unworthy manner will be guilty of the body and blood of the Lord.* [28] But let a man examine himself, and so let him eat of the bread and drink of the cup. *[29] For he who eats and drinks in an unworthy manner eats and drinks judgment to himself, not discerning the Lord's body.* [30] For this reason many are weak and sick among you, and many sleep. (Emphasis Added).

We have already established the fact that the [Blood of Jesus] or the wine, is for the remission of sins. His Blood has paid the price for every sin ever committed and every sin that will ever be committed in the future. If we have received Jesus as Lord and Savior, then we have become new creations in Him.

But what most people don't realize is that Jesus body – the bread – was broken so that we could be made whole. He took the scourging, He bore the penalty for our sins upon Himself: sin, sickness, and disease so that we could be healed.

> [4] Surely, He has borne our griefs (sicknesses, weaknesses, and distresses) and carried our sorrows and pains [of punishment], yet we [ignorantly] considered Him stricken, smitten, and afflicted by God. [5] But He was wounded for our transgressions, He was bruised for our guilt and iniquities; the chastisement [needful to obtain] peace and well-being for us was upon Him, **and with the stripes [that wounded] Him we are healed and made whole.** (Isaiah 53:4-5, AMP, Emphasis Added).

So then, if we look back at 1 Corinthians 11 and what Paul was trying to explain, we find that taking the bread in an "unworthy manner," is to eat it without recognizing that Jesus body was beaten and crucified for our healing.

Paul was saying that when we lump both the bread and the wine together as only a symbol for the forgiveness of our sins – then we are missing out on a crucial provision Jesus has made available to us – OUR HEALING!

Paul says, that because we lump the bread and wine together "NOT DISCERNING" the differences between the bread and wine – for our healing and our forgiveness, we then bring judgement upon ourselves.

In other words, our ignorance to the healing provision Jesus has made available, leads to many people dying needlessly. What we don't know and apply to our lives can kill us.

In Isaiah 55:1 we read, "Everyone who thirsts, come to the waters; and you who have no money, come, buy and eat. Yes, come, buy wine and milk without money and without price."

I encourage you today, to see The Lord's Supper in a whole new light. Understand that Jesus' death was not only for the forgiveness of our sins, but also for the healing of our spirit, soul and body. Healing is yours today if you have made Jesus the Lord of your life.

Get serious about receiving your healing and start taking the communion elements on a daily basis like you would medicine. You can even take three times a day or more if you're led to do so.

And when you partake of the bread, see your sickness being transferred to Jesus on the Cross and His perfect health being transferred to your body. When You drink the juice or the wine, understand that He died so that YOU would be forgiven!

He did it all for YOU! He did it because He loves YOU and because He wants YOU whole in every area of your life. He is *Jehovah Rapha* – The Lord Your Healer! Amen.

Daily Declaration

Thank You Father for Jesus – The Bread of Life! Thank You for Your divine healing, which is actively working mightily in me and restoring me to perfect soundness. I receive all that You have for me: Healing, Wholeness, Blessing, and the Forgiveness of my sins.

From this day forward, I will make a conscious effort to discern the Lord's body each and every time that I partake of the Lord's Supper. I will see my sins on Jesus' body and I will see His healing coming into me.

Thank You Jesus for Healing me. Thank You for taking all of the punishment that I deserve for my sins, upon Yourself. And Thank You for transferring to me, all of the wonderful blessings that rightfully belong to You.

Jesus, You are my Bread of Life. You are the One who has made everything that was bitter, sweet again. You Have empowered me to prosper and taken sickness from my midst. I love You Lord, and I thank You for being My ALL IN ALL! Amen.

Day 29
Ought Not This Daughter Of Abraham Be Loosed Of Her Bonds?

"[11] And behold, there was a woman who had a spirit of infirmity eighteen years, and was bent over and could in no way raise herself up. [12] But when Jesus saw her, He called her to Him and said to her, "Woman, you are loosed from your infirmity." [13] And He laid His hands on her, and immediately she was made straight, and glorified God. [14] But the ruler of the synagogue answered with indignation, because Jesus had healed on the Sabbath; and he said to the crowd, "There are six days on which men ought to work; therefore, come and be healed on them, and not on the Sabbath day." [15] The Lord then answered him and said, "Hypocrite! Does not each one of you on the Sabbath loose his ox or donkey from the stall, and lead it away to water it? [16] So ought not this woman, being a daughter of Abraham, whom Satan has bound—think of it—for eighteen years, be loosed from this bond on the Sabbath?"

Luke 13:11-16

Religion is cold, heartless, and dead, but love, the God kind of love, is compassionate and empathetic. That is why Christianity isn't a religion – it's a love relationship with the Almighty God of Heaven, who is LOVE. (See 1 John 4:8,16). It's a relationship with the Most High God, Whose heart is to see His Children Blessed, Healthy, and Whole. Moreover, we are told in 1 Corinthians chapter 13, that this God Who is LOVE, NEVER FAILS!

"⁴Love endures long and is patient and kind; love never is envious nor boils over with jealousy, is not boastful or vainglorious, does not display itself haughtily. ⁵It is not conceited (arrogant and inflated with pride); it is not rude (unmannerly) and does not act unbecomingly. Love (God's love in us) does not insist on its own rights or its own way, for it is not self-seeking; it is not touchy or fretful or resentful; it takes no account of the evil done to it [it pays no attention to a suffered wrong]. ⁶It does not rejoice at injustice and unrighteousness, but rejoices when right and truth prevail. ⁷Love bears up under anything and everything that comes, is ever ready to believe the best of every person, its hopes are fadeless under all circumstances, and it endures everything [without weakening]. ⁸Love never fails [never fades out or becomes obsolete or comes to an end]. (1 Corinthians 13:4-8, AMP).

Repeatedly, throughout the Gospels we are told that Jesus Who was moved with compassion, healed people who were hurting or in need of healing. Let's look at a few of these stories before moving on.

In Luke chapter 7, Jesus raises a young man from the dead because He had compassion for a widow woman:

¹¹Now it happened, the day after, that He went into a city called Nain; and many of His disciples went with Him, and a large crowd. ¹²And when He came near the gate of the city, behold, a dead man was being carried out, the only son of his mother; and she was a widow. And a large crowd from the city was with her. ¹³ **When the Lord saw her, <u>He had compassion on her</u> and said to her, "Do not weep."** ¹⁴Then He came and touched the open coffin, and those who carried him stood still. And He said, "Young man, I say to you, arise." ¹⁵So he who was dead sat up and began to speak. And He presented him to his mother. (Luke 7:11-13, Emphasis Added).

In Matthew chapter 8, Jesus encounters a leper who knew that Jesus could heal him, but this leper wasn't sure if Jesus would heal him. But Jesus assures the man that He is not only capable, but also willing to heal the him.

> [1]When He had come down from the mountain, great multitudes followed Him. [2]And behold, a leper came and worshiped Him, saying, "Lord, if You are willing, You can make me clean." [3] ***Then Jesus put out His hand and touched him, saying, "I am willing; be cleansed.***" Immediately his leprosy was cleansed. (Matthew 8:1-3, Emphasis Added).

We are repeatedly told that Jesus went from city to city **"HEALING ALL"** who were sick and also healing **EVERY KIND** of sickness and disease. But in Mathew chapter 9, it says that it was because of His compassion for the people.

> [35]Then Jesus went about all the cities and villages, teaching in their synagogues, preaching the gospel of the kingdom, and healing every sickness and every disease among the people. [36] ***But when He saw the multitudes, He was moved with compassion for them***, because they were weary and scattered, like sheep having no shepherd. (Matthew 9:35-36, Emphasis Added).

After the death of His cousin John the Baptist, even in the midst of His own pain and sorrow, Jesus still had compassion on those in need of healing.

> And when Jesus went out He saw a great multitude; ***and He was moved with compassion for them, and healed their sick.*** (Matthew 14:14, Emphasis Added).

29 Now as they went out of Jericho, a great multitude followed Him. 30 And behold, two blind men sitting by the road, when they heard that Jesus was passing by, cried out, saying, "Have mercy on us, O Lord, Son of David!" 31 Then the multitude warned them that they should be quiet; but they cried out all the more, saying, "Have mercy on us, O Lord, Son of David!" 32 So Jesus stood still and called them, and said, "What do you want Me to do for you?" 33 They said to Him, "Lord, that our eyes may be opened." 34 ***So Jesus had compassion and touched their eyes. And immediately their eyes received sight***, and they followed Him. (Matthew 20:29-34, Emphasis Added).

Jesus' compassion is so great that He not only cares about our spiritual and our physical needs, but He also cares about our natural needs too. He cares about the smallest details of our life, including our hunger.

In those days, the multitude being very great and having nothing to eat, Jesus called His disciples to Him and said to them, 2 "***I have compassion on the multitude, because they have now continued with Me three days and have nothing to eat.*** 3 And if I send them away hungry to their own houses, they will faint on the way; for some of them have come from afar." (Mark 8:1-3, Emphasis Added).

Isn't it amazing to know that we have a compassionate and loving God who is concerned with every detail of our lives? I am thrilled to know that He not only hears my cries for Him, but just as with the blind men above, He immediately stops and goes to work righting whatever is wrong in my life.

He's not the kind of God we've been told He is – the absentee father – No! He is very much engaged in every affair we will invite Him into, because He loves us. Hallelujah!

Moreover, our God is a covenant keeping God! All who belong to Him can rest assured, knowing that He will go to battle for us, that He will hear every cry we make asking Him for help, and He will come running to our rescue every time we ask.

We matter to God because we are His covenant children. And just like a protective mother, He won't allow anything or anyone to keep us from His best – and that includes the devil and the religious pawns he uses to try to keep God's people in bondage.

Let's look again at Luke 13:11-16 and see how our compassionate God feels about sickness and disease.

> [11] And behold, there was *a woman who had a spirit of infirmity eighteen years*, and was bent over and could in no way raise herself up. [12] But when Jesus saw her, He called her to Him and said to her, "Woman, you are loosed from your infirmity." [13] And He laid His hands on her, and immediately she was made straight, and glorified God. [14] But the ruler of the synagogue answered with indignation, because Jesus had healed on the Sabbath; and he said to the crowd, "There are six days on which men ought to work; therefore, come and be healed on them, and not on the Sabbath day." [15] The Lord then answered him and said, "Hypocrite! Does not each one of you on the Sabbath loose his ox or donkey from the stall, and lead it away to water it? [16] So *ought not this woman, being a daughter of Abraham, whom Satan has bound—think of it—for eighteen years, be loosed from this bond on the Sabbath?*

First, I want you to notice how long the woman was tormented by "A SPIRIT OF INFIRMITY." The Bible says that this woman had been doubled over for eighteen years. That is 6+6+6, or 666, which is the number of the beast. In other words, it was a demonic spirit that was tormenting this woman.

Second, look at Jesus' response, "ought not this woman, ***being a daughter of Abraham,*** whom Satan has bound—think of it—for eighteen years, be loosed from this bond...?"

Those are covenant words. Jesus is saying, "No covenant child of mine should be remain in bondage to Satan and the Curse!" Abraham was the heir of God's covenant, and the Bible says we are heirs too, if Jesus is our Lord and Savior.

> And if you are Christ's, then you are Abraham's seed, and heirs according to the promise. (Galatians 3:29).

Don't allow the devil to keep you in bondage to sickness, disease, addiction, or any other part of the Curse. Jesus has freed you from that bondage and wants you living Blessed & Whole. If you are a son or a daughter of Abraham through Christ; you've been redeemed from the Curse. (Galatians 3:13-14). And whom the Son sets free, is free indeed! (John 8:36). Hallelujah! Thank You Jesus!

Daily Declaration

Heavenly Father, I am so grateful for Your love and compassion. You love me with an unceasing love. Like John, I know that I am the disciple (the follower of Christ) whom Jesus deeply loves. (See John 13:23, John 19:26, John 20:2, John 21:7, and John 21:20).

Jesus, I know that no matter the trials I face, You are always with me. You will neither leave me nor forsake me, but will see me through to victory.

You have said in Your Word, "⁵I will not in any way fail you nor give you up nor leave you without support. [I will] not, [I will] not, [I will] not in any degree leave you helpless nor forsake nor let [you] down (relax My hold on you)! [Assuredly not!] ⁶ So we take comfort and are encouraged and confidently and boldly say, The Lord is my Helper; I will not be seized with alarm [I will not fear or dread or be terrified]. What can man do to me?" (Hebrews 13:5-6, AMP).

Jesus, Thank You for being true to Your Word. Thank You for being mindful of Your covenant, and for being my God, my Healer, my Provider, my Protector, and everything else I need You to be. You are so good to me and I love You beyond words. I praise You Jesus. Amen.

Day 30
Loaded Down With Blessing & Thriving In Perfect Health

"He brought them forth also with silver and gold: and there was not one feeble person among their tribes."

Psalm 105:37 (KJV)

When we truly pause and pay attention to Scripture, it's easy to see the heart of God for His people. Too many people view God as a hard task master, who is just waiting for one slip up, so that He can punish us, but that's not who our God is. He is a loving Father; whose heart is to see us BLESSED and paid back for all of the injustices done to us by the enemy.

I love the story of the Hebrew exodus from Egypt. It's not only a story of liberation, but a story of triumph over satanic forces, and a story of God's Blessing in operation, for those He covenanted to be their God.

The story begins with the Hebrew nation living as slaves in Egypt after the death of Joseph. The new Pharaoh who had recently come to power, didn't honor Joseph, a Hebrew slave, who was made the Vizier (the highest-ranking official under Pharaoh), of Egypt. As a result, this new Pharaoh was cruel to the Hebrew nation, he made them slaves, treated them like animals, and forced them to build cities to show off his wealth and power.

But as time passed, God raised up a deliverer named Moses, who would eventually lead God's people back to their homeland after 400 years of slavery in Egypt.

There was a problem however, Pharaoh didn't want his workforce to just get up and leave. That would mean that he needed to find new workers to do his bidding, and the Egyptians were comfortable – lazy – living off the backs of the Hebrew slaves. Therefore, Pharaoh refused to allow the Hebrews to leave – that was until God brought 10 plagues upon Egypt – which eventually led to the death of Pharaoh's firstborn son.

Brokenhearted and exhausted from opposing God, Pharaoh finally agrees to let the Hebrew people leave Egypt and go back to their homeland – the Promised land.

Now that you have the background to the exodus, let's back up and see how God instructed the Hebrews before the Passover.

[3] Speak to all the congregation of Israel, saying: …every man shall take for himself a lamb, according to the house of his father, a lamb for a household. [4] And if the household is too small for the lamb, let him and his neighbor next to his house take it according to the number of the persons… [5] **Your lamb shall be without blemish**, a male of the first year. You may take it from the sheep or from the goats… [6] Then the whole assembly of the congregation of Israel shall kill it at twilight. [7] And they shall take some of the blood and put it on the two doorposts and on the lintel of the houses where they eat it. [8] **Then they shall eat the flesh on that night; roasted in fire**, with unleavened bread and with bitter herbs they shall eat it. [9] **Do not eat it raw, nor boiled at all with water, but roasted in fire—its head with its legs and its entrails. [10] You shall let none of it remain until morning**, and what remains of it until morning you shall burn with fire. [11] And thus you shall eat it: with a belt on your waist, your sandals on your feet, and your staff in your hand. So, you shall eat it in haste. It is the LORD's Passover. [12] 'For I will pass through the land of Egypt on that night, and will strike all the firstborn in the land of Egypt, both man and beast; and against all the gods of Egypt I will execute judgment: I am the LORD. [13] **Now the blood shall be a sign for you on the houses where you are. And when I see the blood, I will pass over you; and**

the plague shall not be on you to destroy you when I strike the land of Egypt. (Exodus 12:3-12, Emphasis Added).

In a message by Joseph Prince called *Supernatural Health Through The Roasted Lamb*, he outlines some important facts that have really helped me understand what took place during the very first Passover.

We must first remember that Jesus is the unblemished Lamb of God, who was slain for our salvation (wholeness in every area – spirit, soul, and body).

John refers to Jesus as the Lamb of God saying, "Behold! The Lamb of God who takes away the sin of the world!" (John 1:29).

In Revelation 13:8, the Apostle again refers to Jesus as the Lamb of God who was slain from the foundation of the world.

Joseph Prince suggests that when God instructed the Hebrews to eat the Passover lamb, "roasted by fire," that it was symbolism for Jesus, who would willingly be "roasted by the wrath of God," in order to pay for humanity's sin. Sin demands judgement! And Jesus paid the full penalty for our sin on the Cross.

Exodus 12:9 says, "Do not eat it raw, nor boiled at all with water, but roasted in fire—its head with its legs and its entrails. [10] You shall let none of it remain until morning."

Prince makes a great point saying that in Chinese medicine, they believe in the theory of "part for part," meaning if you have liver problems, you eat the liver of an animal, if you have heart problems, you eat the animals heart. By doing so, it is believed that the animal's liver or heart will make your liver or heart healthy. That healing comes to a person simply by eating the part of the animal that is ailing in your own body.

Think about it for a moment. Sin, sickness, and disease came as the result of eating something in the Garden. Why can't it be reversed though eating something else – The Lord's Body?

What do people do if they are bitten by a poisonous snake? The doctor injects them with the anti-venom (more of the same poison), to counteract the effects of the poison with more poison.

The same is true with vaccinations. Vaccines are made from small amounts of pathogenic viruses that the doctor injects into us to help us develop immunity to those viruses or diseases.

Where does this idea originate? It originates from the Bible. In Numbers 21, when the Israelites were complaining against Moses and ultimately against God, poisonous snakes bit them and many of them died.

> So, Moses made a bronze serpent, and put it on a pole; and so, it was, if a serpent had bitten anyone, when he looked at the bronze serpent, he lived. (Numbers 21:9).

The serpent on the pole is another foreshadow of the work that Jesus would do for all Humanity, redeeming us from our sins on the Cross. Though Jesus isn't the serpent, the serpent on the pole represents sin and its originator – Satan, and ultimately his defeat on the Cross.

We must get to the point where we can see our sins, sicknesses, and diseases judged in the body of Jesus on the Cross. Once we do, sickness cannot remain in us.

God will not punish the same sin twice. We have adopted this practice into our own judicial system. We call it double jeopardy, and this law stipulates that a person can only be tried and punished for a crime one time and one time only.

ALL sin, sickness, and disease has been dealt with once and for all in the body of Jesus. He took it ALL, and He bore the wrath of God's judgement in His sinless and righteous body. As a result, His righteousness has been transferred to all who will believe on Him as Lord and Savior. Sin, sickness, and condemnation, no longer have a legitimate claim to us – we have been REDEEMED!

We are told, "[37] Then the children of Israel journeyed from Rameses to Succoth, about six hundred thousand men on foot, besides children. [38] A mixed multitude went up with them also, and flocks and herds—a great deal of livestock." (Exodus 12:37-38).

You've got to remember that the 600,000 only represent the men twenty years old and older, not the women or the children. Scholars suggest that the total number of Hebrews leaving Egypt was somewhere between 2-3 million.

Moreover, the Bible says, "He brought them forth also with silver and gold: ***and there was not one feeble person among their tribes.***" (Psalm 105:37, Emphasis Added).

So, when exodus 12:9 says that God told them to eat the lamb roasted, the head, the entrails, legs and all. These Hebrew slaves were in a sense, eating the Body of Christ as we spoke about in yesterday's devotion.

Those who were old and had bad eyesight probably ate the eyes of the lamb. Those with a weak heart ate the heart of the lamb. And those who were just old and feeble from years of malnutrition, hard labor, and abuse as slaves, ate the legs and other parts of the lamb and became strong.

Think about it. Psalm 105:37 explicitly tells us that God brought them out rich – with the gold and silver the Egyptians gave them to leave their country ***AND THERE WAS NOT ONE FEEBLE AMONG THEM!***

In other words, God supernaturally renewed the youth of each and every one of the 3 million Hebrews that came out of Egypt. No one needed a cane to walk. No one needed a wagon or cart to ride in – they were all strong and healthy for the journey to the Promised land.

Not only did God do it for the Hebrews in Egypt, but He will do it for YOU too. The Bible tells us that God is no respecter of persons, if He did it for one, He'll do for everyone who will believe Him. (Acts 10:34, Romans 2:11).

So, if you are dealing with any kind of sickness and disease, it's time to start seeing that sickness on the body of Jesus. He is the roasted Lamb of God, Who bore the wrath of God's judgement in His body, so that you and I don't have to. God will not make you pay for any sin or sickness that Jesus has already bore. You have been redeemed form the Curse and made the righteousness of God in Christ!

I encourage you to take the time today to get the communion elements: bread and wine or juice, and take them, remembering what the Lord Jesus has done for you. As you do, close your eyes and envision that sickness upon Jesus' body.

If it has something to do with your eyes, then as you take the communion elements do like the Hebrews did during the first Passover, and see yourself eating the eyes of the lamb and your eyes being restored to 2020 vision. You can do the same thing no matter what part of your body needs healing, all it takes is faith and a willing heart. When you do, I believe God will honor your faith and make you whole – IN JESUS' NAME. AMEN!

Daily Declaration

Abba Father, I thank You for Your Perfect Health flowing throughout my body. Every cell, tissue, organ, bone, and fiber of my being is being rejuvenated and made perfectly sound, even as I pray this prayer to You.

As I worship You today, and take the Lord's Supper, I know that Your healing power is flowing to me – making all things new and restoring me to perfect health.

Just like the Hebrew slaves that You brought out of captivity, rich in silver, rich in gold, and rich in health, so that there was not even one feeble among their clan, I receive that same healing anointing in my own body.

Father, I know that **_ALL_** of my sins, **_ALL_** of my shortcomings, and **_ALL_** sickness and disease have been judged in the body of Jesus! I have been redeemed from Your wrath, redeemed from the kingdom of darkness and translated into the glorious love of Your Son, Jesus. (See Colossians 1:13). I am no longer fearful about tomorrow. I know my God. I know the love of my Father and the love of my Lord and Savior, Jesus. I can confidently proclaim:

> [For it is He] Who delivered and saved me and called me with a calling... [He did it] not because of anything of merit that I have done, but because of His grace (unmerited favor) which was given to me in Christ Jesus before the world began [eternal ages ago]. [It is that purpose and grace] which He now has made known and has fully disclosed and made real [to me] through the appearing of my Savior Christ Jesus, Who annulled death and made it of no effect and brought life and immortality (immunity from eternal death) to light through the Gospel...And this is why...I am not ashamed, for I know (perceive, have knowledge of, and am acquainted with) Him Whom I have believed (adhered to and trusted in and relied on), and I am [positively] persuaded that He is able to guard and keep that which has been entrusted to me and which I have committed [to Him] until that day. (2 Timothy 1:9-12, AMP). Amen!

Day 31
As He Is, So Am I In This World.

"…As He is, so are we in this world."

1 John 4:17

Whe know who we are IN CHRIST: and ALL that we have access to, and ALL that we have been delivered from because of Jesus' substitutional sacrifice on the Cross, we become bold in our faith and we begin to walk in the authority our Heavenly Father intended for us to walk in, as Kings and Priests of the Most High God.

The life of the believer is not meant to be a life of do, do, do. The "good works" that we do are the byproduct of our faith and love for Jesus. They are the natural response to His love which has been manifested towards us. No, the life of the believer is realizing that everything you and I have need of, has already been DONE – IN JESUS.

Sin has been defeated! The Curse has been broken! Our freedom has been established! And now, our job as believers, is to share the love of Jesus with others and to REST IN HIS FINISHED WORK!

When fear comes, **WE REST** knowing that we have been delivered from fear and we remind the devil that God has not given us the spirit of fear. When sickness tries to rear its ugly head, **WE REST** knowing that Jesus has defeated sickness and disease on the Cross of Calvary, and by His stripes we've been healed. Every time the enemy comes trying to hand out His trash, we give him the Word of God concerning that matter, and **WE REST** in confidence, knowing that God loves us and that He's at work perfecting everything that concerns us.

The Bible tells us that the work that the believer is to do is a work of faith and rest. Rest comes from the highest level of faith. Even when bad things are happening all around us, faith says, "Lord, I see and hear all of this commotion going on around me, but I am not moved by what I see and hear. I am only moved by Your Word and my understanding of Jesus authority over my circumstances. I choose to rest in that knowledge, understanding that You will see me through, in Jesus' name."

The Bible says, "Let us labor therefore to enter into that rest, lest any man fall after the same example of unbelief." (Hebrews 10:11, KJV).

I want to share another story that I heard from pastor Joseph Prince out of Singapore. He shared a story about how he had been preaching on 1 John 4:17 which says, "Love has been perfected among us in this: that we may have boldness in the day of judgment; *because **AS HE IS, SO ARE WE IN THIS WORLD.***" (Emphasis Added).

He told how for years he had been teaching on this verse concerning our standing in Christ Jesus. That because Jesus dealt with sin on the Cross, we have been made the righteousness of God in Him (2 Corinthians 5:21). Sin no longer has dominion over us.

But in recent years, the Lord had been dealing with him concerning this Scripture and the healing provision Jesus has made for us – that by His stripes ***we ARE healed***.

As a result, pastor Prince began teaching that as Jesus is now: seated at the right hand of the Father in Heaven, perfectly healed, perfectly whole, strong, and lacking no good thing, so are we – IN HIM.

Soon afterwards, testimonies began flooding in to Joseph Prince Ministries telling about the signs and wonders God was doing all over the world because of this teaching. People who had been facing terminal diseases – diseases that doctors said were incurable – had begun to see themselves healed, whole, and thriving.

One lady in China wrote to pastor Prince saying that after hearing his sermon *AS HE IS SO ARE WE IN THIS WORLD*, she went in to her doctor for a routine mammogram. Later that day, she received a message that she needed to return straightaway. When she arrived, she was informed that she had a mass which was most definitely malignant and needed to be removed immediately.

This woman, shaken from the news, walked out of the doctor's office with the medical report still in her hand, and got into her car. As she sat in her car fighting back fear, she took out a pen and wrote these words on the medical report: *Lord Jesus, You don't have breast cancer in Your body, and as You are, so am I in You.*

When this woman went back to her doctor (I believe it was later the same day), she asked the doctor to take another mammogram of the same breast. When he did, the cancerous mass had supernaturally dissolved and disappeared. Hallelujah!

Another woman from New York, wrote in to give her testimony about her healed knees. She told how she had been diagnosed with severe osteoarthritis. She could no longer kneel due to intense pain and discomfort. She described how she experienced difficulty climbing stairs and even raising herself from a seated position. The arthritis had finally gotten to the point where she needed physical therapy. But after thirteen weeks of therapy she still had no relief.

She told how after hearing pastor Prince's message she began confessing that as Jesus is, so is she in this world, and miraculously the arthritis was healed, and she was pain free. She shared that she was now serving other senior friends by bending down and doing things for them that they couldn't do. Praise Jesus!

I'm sharing these testimonies with you as an illustration demonstrating that NOTHING IS IMPOSSIBLE for those who will believe God and His precious promises in the Bible. Healing belongs to you in Jesus. Everything that you have need of, has already been made available to you IN HIM. Your job is to receive it by faith and rest knowing that it must manifest in your life if you don't throw away your confidence.

Hebrews 10:35-36 says, "[35] Therefore do not cast away your confidence, which has great reward. [36] For you have need of endurance [patience], so that after you have done the will of God [rested], you may receive the promise."

The Bible also tells us, "*9 Therefore God also has highly exalted Him [Jesus] __and given Him the name which is above every name, 10 that at the name of Jesus every knee should bow, of those in heaven, and of those on earth, and of those under the earth,__ 11 and that every tongue should confess that Jesus Christ is Lord, to the glory of God the Father." (Philippians 2:9-11, Emphasis Added).

I want you to know, cancer, diabetes, MRSA, bird flu, arthritis, etc., are all names. Jesus has a name that is greater than ALL of those names. At the name of Jesus, cancer must bow and leave your body. Diabetes must bow and flee.

But if you don't establish your authority IN Christ, and if you just remain complacent and timid – these diseases will remain. You've got to rise up, get mad, and command them to leave your body in the MIGHTY NAME OF JESUS! He's already defeated them on the Cross – Your job is to establish that defeat by washing your mind with the Word of God (See Ephesians 5:26), and start confessing out loud what rightfully belongs to you IN CHRIST.

Another thing that will help you establish your authority and belief in YOUR perfect health in Jesus, is to ask the question: "Lord Jesus, do you have _____ condition in Your body? And Then begin to say, Lord, You don't have _____, and the Bible says that as You are, so am I in THIS WORLD! Amen.

Jesus, as you do Your perfect work in me, I am determined to do the work You have called me to do, which is to believe Your holy Word and to labor to enter into Your rest.

Thank You Lord for being a Good God! Thank You for being a Man of Your Word and for doing what You have promised to do. I receive my healing and perfect soundness right now, in Jesus' mighty name, AMEN!

Daily Declaration

Father, I thank You that Your divine healing is working mightily in my body today and every day going forward. I declare that sickness and disease have no authority or power in my life because Jesus bore my sickness and carried my diseases on the Cross. _____, must bow its knee to the name of Jesus and flee this instant, in Jesus' mighty name.

Lord, I see myself healed, whole and delivered in Jesus mighty name. No weapon formed against me shall prosper. I plead the blood of Jesus over everything that concerns me. His blood has cleansed me from every effect of the Curse. No sin, sickness, or plague can harm me in any way.

The Bible promises, [6] "Blessed shall you be when you come in, and blessed shall you be when you go out. [7] "The LORD will cause your enemies who rise against you to be defeated before your face; they shall come out against you one way and flee before you seven ways. [8] "***The LORD will command the blessing on you*** in your storehouses and in all to which you set your hand... (Deuteronomy 28:6-8, Emphasis Added).

If God has BLESSED me, then who can curse me? The answer is no one! Even the evil prophet Balaam could not curse the people of God for profit. God sent him back to king Balak saying:

> How shall I curse whom God has not cursed? And how shall I denounce whom the LORD has not denounced? ...Behold, I have received a command to bless; He has blessed, and I cannot reverse it. (See Numbers 23:8, 20).

In the name of Jesus, I stand on the sure promises of the Bible and I claim my healing and wholeness, IN JESUS' NAME! I rest in the fact that Jesus has delivered me from the dominion of Satan and As He is, so am I in this world! Amen.

Made in the USA
Columbia, SC
23 August 2018